Pilgrims
Searching for a Home

The Odyssey of a Family

Carl E. Hansen

WestBow Press books may be ordered through booksellers or by contacting:

WestBow Press
A Division of Thomas Nelson & Zondervan
1663 Liberty Drive
Bloomington, IN 47403
www.westbowpress.com
844-714-3454

Cover designed by Destiny Kreider of "Destiny Designs", a granddaughter of the author

ISBN: 978-1-6642-7200-2 (sc)
ISBN: 978-1-6642-7201-9 (hc)
ISBN: 978-1-6642-7199-9 (e)

Library of Congress Control Number: 2022912698

Print information available on the last page.

WestBow Press rev. date: 10/05/2022

Dedication

To all those who come behind us, and especially to those, our grandchildren: Jasmine Marie Bundick, Carlin Hans Kreider, Destiny Joy Kreider, Desta Ashe Hansen, Kierston Shane Kreider, Justus Angelo Payne, Oriana Danae Kreider, Isaiah Payne and Darius Blakeley.

And to our greatgrandchildren: Arden Joash Kreider, Jaron Mathis Kreider, Riah Nashae Kreider, Tyrus Jesai Kreider and Zaya Jael Kreider.

And to those yet unborn, who follow us in their pilgrimages; that they might remember from whence they have come, and so better understand who they are, and where they are going.

We're pilgrims on the journey of the narrow road
And those who've gone before us line the way
Cheering on the faithful, encouraging the weary.
Their lives a stirring testament to God's sustaining grace.

Surrounded by so great a cloud of witnesses,
Let us run the race not only for the prize,
But as those who've gone before us, let us leave to those behind us
The heritage of faithfulness passed on through godly lives.

– "Find Us Faithful" by Jon Mohr, Publisher,
Birdwing Music, 1987

Contents

Foreword

This book has been in incubation for many years. It was in a high school English Composition class sixty-four years ago that the idea first entered my head that someday I must write a history of my family. After drafting a one-page beginning, I reverted to my built-in habit of procrastination. Through the years I collected tidbits of historical information with good intentions.

It was in the fall of 1991, having returned as a "burned out" missionary from Kenya with a full year sabbatical on my hands to do with as I pleased, that I determined that now the time had finally come.

But writing a book wasn't that simple. There were the technical aspects. I was convinced that first, I must buy one of those new contraptions called a "personal computer" that had miraculously taken over the western world while I was vegetating in the Maasai bush. Unfortunately, the knowledge of its use didn't come with the price. I would have to learn to use the headstrong thing. Furthermore, I would have to learn the basic art of typing. So, I started my race from a hundred paces behind the starting line.

First, I carefully selected the "right" computer, a simple Toshiba laptop with twenty megabytes hard drive and the DOS operating system. By the time I took two weeks' worth of computer classes, typed a few practice letters, and a booklet for my Mission, it was mid-December before I got started on this project. By the time my furlough had run out, I had a rough draft of about 250 pages of collected material and my own memories that could be sorted into several different books.

I returned to Kenya to a new and challenging assignment. But I did periodically find spare time to continue compiling a record of my family's collective memories. Out of this growing collection, I managed to put together, and have self-published and printed, by Masthof Press in 1998, this story of my grandparents, *"Jacob and Justina: Pilgrims – The Odyssey of a Family."*

It has been twenty-four years since the book was published. In the intervening years, changes have taken place, new information has come to light, and the story needed some corrections. Further, since I am in the process of writing four additional autobiographical books on the various phases of Vera's and my own pilgrimage as missionaries, I thought it time to re-publish this book. I thought it wise to reshape this volume to fit the additional four, making a set of five books, and have them all published together.

Acknowledgements

Above all, I want to express my gratitude to God for a good heritage, for godly ancestors and for a story worth writing about. Also, for the gift of time, the opportunity, the ability, and the stamina to write it. Our history is really *His-story*!

For the material in this book, I am deeply indebted to several persons. Without their help, I would never have uncovered the detailed information contained in this book.

Of first importance, I am indebted to my now late mother, Elizabeth Winifred (Friesen) Hansen, who was an eyewitness and participant in much of the story. She had been recording information throughout her years, and in her early sixties, learned to type, on a simple typewriter, and wrote about 40 single-spaced typed pages of her memories.

These collected memories and the fruits of her research, she passed on to me, her second born, and the only one with a predisposition to become the "family historian." These provided me with a good starting point. She kindly proof-read my manuscript and suggested some corrections for my first edition. She also provided, from her personal collection, most of the pictures reproduced in this book.

Secondly, I am deeply indebted to my late aunt, Tena June Friesen, who also passed on to me a copy of her memories, an unpublished manuscript of 284 double-spaced typed pages, laboriously and lovingly typed and illustrated with her own sketches. She provided me with a "second witness," a set of younger eyes through which to evaluate my mother's perceptions.

With these two witnesses, I began to put together the shell of the story. Then I checked with some of my other aunts and uncles, now deceased, especially my aunts, Helen Biehn, Esther Visser, Susan Friesen, and Annie

Roth, and my uncle, Jake Friesen, and others who contributed anecdotes and information about their families.

I am also indebted to my late aunt, Hedy Friesen, who, through the years, faithfully compiled and updated a record of the family tree.

Finally, I thank my faithful wife and partner, Vera, for proofreading this manuscript and offering helpful suggestions. Besides, I owe her an unpayable debt for the many lonely evenings she spent by herself and going to the cold bed alone, while I slowly pecked away on the keyboard. She still loves me!

I take full responsibility for any errors or omissions that may offend other witnesses. I received a lot of encouragement and cooperation from some of the members of the family, while others were indifferent or silent. If there are other opinions or different viewpoints, let them be charitable towards my efforts. It was not without purpose that we have the four Gospels, four witnesses to the one life of Christ. So, in this story, let others give their witness!

For this second edition, I would love to have visited Russia, did more research into the early history of the ancestors, but the opportunity did not present itself. Time is passing, one's powers fade, I think I have procrastinated enough. Let me give my witness now and leave it to future historians of another era to dig deeper if they so choose.

Carl Edward Hansen
1523 Park Road
Harrisonburg, Virginia, USA
June 14, 2022

Acronyms

CPR	Canadian Pacific Railroad
CO	Conscientious Objector
EID	Eastern Irrigation District
EMC	Eastern Mennonite College
EMBMC	Eastern Mennonite Board of Missions and Charities
EMM	Eastern Mennonite Mission
MCC	Mennonite Central Committee
RCMP	Royal Canadian Mounted Police
USSR	Union of Soviet Socialist Republics

Introduction

In rare moments of deep reflection, I am profoundly impressed by the relativity of all things in our universe. Outside on a clear dark night, one can glance across a good portion of the universe and move on, thinking that the universe, though very vast and quite populated with stars, is yet quite simple and comprehensible. One might allow oneself to be deceived into thinking that the reality that one has seen is all there is to that reality.

But the wise people who study the stars with their computerized electronic telescopes tell us that the light we see tonight from the nearest visible star, Proxima Centauri, began its journey through space four years and one hundred and nine days ago, travelling at five thousand, eight hundred and eighty billion (5,880,000,000,000) miles per year. In comparison our Sun's light reaches us in eight minutes.

They tell us that the light, we see emanating from the furthest visible star, left it's source millions of years ago; and those stars in reality are not there anymore as we see them, for they have long since moved on in their journey with the ever expanding universe; and some of them have burned out and imploded into super dense cold invisible black holes, which suck up the debris and even the light rays that travel past in the vast reaches of outer space.

They say that Betelgeuse, the brightest star in Orion, which looks so little and cold, is really a giant burning nuclear furnace with interior temperatures reaching millions of degrees; and though it appears so small, its diameter is 400 times as large as that of our Sun, or slightly larger than the whole diameter of the orbit of Mars.

They tell us that the universe used to be empty, entirely void of matter. Then, at one moment in one place, electrons mysteriously flashed into relationship with a "Big Bang." That cosmic explosion flung newly created matter in every direction.

They say there is evidence to indicate that matter, including our solar system and galaxy, is still travelling ever outward at the same rate of speed and in the same direction as it began so many billions of years ago.

We can only see approximately 4,000 stars, looking from both sides of our planet with our naked eyes. However, those with the best telescopes can see over three billion (3,000,000,000) individual stars plus over one billion (1,000,000,000) galaxies with billions of stars in each, or approximately two hundred billion billion (200,000,000,000,000,000,000) stars in total.

They tell us that most of them, like our sun, are orbited by planets, some of which may possibly be able to sustain life, like our planet earth.

Likewise, we can learn from the physicist about the inner space in our world of matter. He will tell you that the solid and liquid and air matter that we know to be real, is mostly space. A thing as simple as a common rock is really an intricate structure of billions of atoms stuck equidistant from each other in rigid patterns held in place by strong electrostatic forces generated by electrons spinning billions of orbits around a nucleus of neutrons and protons in a millionth of a second.

He would explain that there are as many atoms in two drops of water as there are estimated stars in the known universe (200,000,000,000,000,000,000), each drop a miniature universe and each atom a miniature solar system.

He would tell you that the electron is so small and there is so much empty inner space in what we know as matter, that it would be possible, if it were to travel in a straight line, for an electron to pass through our earth seven times without striking anything, not even another electron. Perhaps this can help us to begin to understand why x-rays can pass through our body, without us feeling anything but the cold steel that our bare skin is laying on.

In fact, the physicist will tell you that, if all the inner space of our mother earth were removed, and only the protons, neutrons, and electrons, which make up all the earth's atoms, were collapsed together, they could fit into a common bushel basket. But you couldn't carry it, for it would still weigh the same as our whole earth does now. It would be another "black hole", a cosmic vacuum cleaner sucking in all the asteroidal debris and light rays that came near it's gravitational pull.

In fact, the existence of all matter can be reduced to a relationship between electricity and space and time.

The "Big Bang" introduced relationship between electricity and space at a specific moment in eternal time. At that historic moment when God spoke the creative word, the universe came into being, electrons, protons, and neutrons relating to one another in 118 distinct combinations forming the elements, the basic building blocks of which our whole material universe is constructed.

Reflecting upon these existences, from the absolute smallness of the electron to the enormity of a Betelgeuse or the incomprehensible vastness of our universe, one gets a sense of the utter relativity of space and time that makes up the total of existence. One might ask with the sufferer, "What is man that you make so much of him, that you give him so much attention?" (Job 7:17)

Indeed, we humans live in a microcosm, a planet greenhouse, a sheltered little speck in a hostile universe of vast spaces of absolute zero-degree temperatures separated from inferno suns of more than forty million (40,000,000) degrees. Our "three score years and ten" is but a millisecond on the eternal time clock.

Yet in our own speck of space and millisecond of time, each one of us is infinitely important. Our birth is anxiously awaited by our parents. Our photographs are taken, and our weight is recorded and announced to all who care, and to many who don't. The government makes a record of our entrance. We are "ooohhhed" and "aaahhhed" over.

Our first semblances of speech are excitedly repeated, in distorted adult accents, to any and all who will listen. Our progress is carefully monitored by family and the medical profession. Our birthdays are remembered and celebrated. Clothing and toys and food are lavished upon us.

We are forced to go to school and the dentist "for your own good!" Our graduation is eagerly anticipated and celebrated.

We marry, raise a family, work hard, build a house or maybe an industrial empire, plant flowers or trees, maybe write books or paint pictures. We learn, think, believe, feel, love, hate, are tempted, sin, repent, and grow.

We struggle to make a living for ourselves and our family. Sometimes we fail and suffer disappointment. Sometimes we succeed and enjoy the fruits of our efforts. We endure hard times and enjoy good times.

We celebrate and rejoice with friends. We suffer loss and weep alone. We make mistakes that we may or may not be able to rectify. We do acts of heroism, large or small, that may go unnoticed or be praised and recorded in histories or remembered in legends.

However, at the end of our millisecond, we will die. Tears will be shed, and eulogies made; flowers will be interred with our more or less splendid casket; a stone may be erected with our name etched in granite, and perhaps, if we are lucky, a fitting epitaph.

But our body will molder into dust, and our memory will be forgotten long before the name is weathered from the stone. Children, of another millisecond, may play among the stones and speak once more our weathered name, but it will be only cold, dull, meaningless syllables, devoid of any warmth of blood and flesh or sigh of hopes and desires or sweat of struggles and achievements.

It is with the intention to prolong their fading memory, that I undertake to write this story of a peasant couple of an expired millisecond, by reattaching the warmth of flesh and blood to the weathering granite of their name; that unborn descendants of a future millisecond might hear, ever so faintly, their voices speaking of courage and faith, of love and commitment; and smell their sweat and feel their pain as they struggled against adverse elements that sought to defeat them; and watch and learn from them the art of living, of coping with hardships and keeping a song of gratitude in their hearts, and a smile of hospitality on their faces, and an encouraging word on their lips, triumphing over despair.

I have only known my maternal grandfather and grandmother, Jacob and Justina Friesen as old people, although they were still bearing children when I was born, and hence were not old at all. Yet, they seemed old to the little boy who knew them as "Gramma" and "Grampa."

Their sufferings through war and famine in Russia, and their hard toil in forcing a living out of the dust bowl soil of western Canada, during the "dirty thirties," had stooped their bodies and bronzed and wrinkled their skin, and enhanced their inherited peasant bearing, and made them to appear older than they in fact were.

Grandfather stood at about five feet and eight inches tall and, in his prime, weighed between 180 and 190 lbs. He was of solid build, with large chest and protruding abdomen, and had big hands and feet. His sturdy head was crowned with a heavy set of light brown hair which he wore cropped short and usually uncombed, giving him that home-barbered unkempt peasant look. Dark brown eyes peered from below his worry-creased forehead and bushy eyebrows. A broad straight nose, and thick lips, long since frozen in a natural sober frown on a square firm-set jaw complimented his deep-tanned wind-burned face. One would usually find him dressed in denim overalls or dark beltless trousers with suspenders, and a warm plaid flannel shirt with long sleeves and buttoned up to the top.

Grandmother was a medium sized woman of about five feet and four inches in height, and about 140 lbs. Her slightly stooped body showed the evidence of having birthed fourteen healthy children in twenty-three years while laboring hard in field and garden to feed them and care for them through the tough depression years, all of this while moving, on the average, once every eighteen months.

She wore her grey-streaked brown hair combed back and tied in a bun at the base of her head. Her face was refined, with thin lips, and slightly curved-out nose. Prominent cheek bones accentuated her perpetual smile. Glasses partially concealed small friendly smiling eyes. Her teeth were worn and showing signs of decay. Her skin was weathered and creased with the cares and demands imposed upon her by the years.

She dressed in the modest styles and somber colors without benefit of accessories or cosmetics, as was fitting a woman of her age and time and peasant class. She loved her children and grandchildren and always had a warm word for us. She was a woman of deep faith and prayer and was an inspiration to all her family, and those in the community who knew her.

The millisecond of this couple's sojourn in our little greenhouse speck in the vast universe has passed some time ago. They were pilgrims "tenting" their way through this life. They never became rich or famous. They never accumulated estates or built mansions. They died as they lived, moving on in search for a city that has permanent foundations whose architect and builder is God.

O Lord, our Lord,
How majestic is your name
in all the earth!
You have set your glory
above the heavens.

When I consider your heavens,
the work of your fingers,
the moon and the stars,
which you have set in place.
What is man that you are mindful of him,
the son of man that you care for him?

You made him a little lower
than the heavenly beings
and crowned him with glory and honor.
You made him ruler over
the works of your hands.
You put everything under his feet!

– Psalms 8:1, 3-6 (NIV)

1

Searching for Utopia

> *By faith Abraham, when called to go to a place he would later receive as his inheritance, obeyed, and went, even though he did not know where he was going. By faith, he made his home in the promised land, like a stranger in a foreign country; he lived in tents, as did Isaac and Jacob, who were heirs with him of the same promise. For he was looking forward to the city with foundations, whose architect and builder is God.* – Hebrews 11:8-10 NIV.

Jacob and Justina Friesen's ancestors were among that group of people called "Russian Mennonites" or sometimes "German Mennonites." But they were, in fact, really "Dutch Mennonites." People with names like "Warkentin," "Huebert," and "Friesen" originally came from Friesland, in northern Holland. Sometime after 1530, they became participants in the Anabaptist renewal movement that swept through Holland, north and south Germany, Switzerland, Alsace-Lorraine, and much of Austria.

In Holland they became known as "Mennists" and later "Mennonites." Those were intolerant times, and religious deviation was not allowed in most princedoms. The Anabaptists were hated everywhere and persecuted in most places. When the persecution intensified in one administrative region and too many lost their lives, the remaining believers would emigrate to another district, where there was a climate of tolerance.

Already in the 1530's, Mennonites began migrating from Holland to the commercial city of Danzig in Poland, where there was more toleration for their religious views and opportunities to support themselves in the trades.

The migration intensified after 1562, when the persecution in Holland got severe. The Polish rulers offered them unused swamp land, in the delta of the Vistula River, if they would develop it. In turn the Poles promised that their Anabaptist religious views would be tolerated, and that their sons would be exempted from the duty to bear arms.

And of course, the Dutch Frieslanders knew how to drain swamps better than anyone else in the world. Soon their community prospered and their numbers grew.

In time, after the territory passed from Polish rule to Prussian rule, the German language and culture gradually dominated.

The Mennonites adjusted to the German language, which was used in church and school while they maintained their East Friesland vernacular, "Plattdeutsch," a Dutch-German dialect, for everyday use. They incorporated some elements of the Germanic culture into their own, but at the same time, they maintained a distinct separateness from the culture and the people around them.

After living in Prussia for about two hundred years, the colony of Dutch Mennonites had become quite large, prosperous, and sophisticated. In the meantime, the Prussian military spirit was on the rise. The Mennonite people with their commitment to a non-military, non-patriotic, and non-resistant way of life, didn't fit the popular prevailing sentiments of the times.

Their tranquil lifestyle came under threat when the Kaiser decided to waive the right of exemption from military service for all Mennonite men. From now on, they would be subject to the draft like everybody else. Young men were also restricted from buying land unless they had served in the military. This was very threatening to the Mennonites who were being squeezed on their land because of rapid natural growth.

Some of them began to look elsewhere for a haven where they could have freedom to live according to the dictates of their consciences, as shaped by their religious beliefs.

Finding a "Promised Land" in Russia

> *I have indeed seen the misery of my people in Egypt. I have heard them crying out because of their slave drivers, and I am concerned about their suffering. So, I have come down to rescue them from the hand of the Egyptians and to bring them up out*

> *of that land into a good and spacious land, a land flowing with milk and honey.* – Exodus 3:7-8 NIV

In 1786, the Empress of Russia, Catherine II, sometimes called "The Great," offered such a haven. She offered the Mennonites a safe home, in the then sparsely inhabited and undeveloped steppes of southern Ukraine and other parts of southern Russia. They would be free to develop their own colonies, maintain their own culture and language, have their own schools, worship as they wished, govern their own affairs, and be exempt from military service. The rich, virgin land was free, and loans for travel expenses were promised. The offer was too good for some to resist.

In Prussia, to preserve their dissenting religious beliefs and practices of "separation from the world," the Mennonites adopted the communal lifestyle of living in colonies.

This practice was continued in Russia. Each colony consisted of a cluster of villages. Each village was made up of several households or homesteads, each of which had a piece of land for a garden. The village also had a school and a mill. The schoolhouse also served as a church meeting house. The land surrounding each village was parceled out to those in the village. For major celebrations, such as Pentecost, baptism, and communion, the worshipers, from each of the villages, went to the big church, in the center of the colony.

In 1788, 228 Mennonite families emigrated to southern Ukraine and established the first settlement called Chortitza. Eventually, 462 Prussian Mennonite families settled there, forming eighteen villages comprising 113,000 acres. In 1803, a second settlement at Molotschna was established with 150 families. Then followed two settlements in Samara Province (now Kuybyshev), in the middle Volga region—first Trakt, in 1853, then Alexandertal or Old Samara, in 1859.

These flourishing colonies spread out to other regions of the Russian Empire. By 1914, these had expanded to fifty-four settlements. They had 365 villages with about 110,000 Mennonites engaged in many kinds of productive businesses and farming four million acres of prime land.

The farms prospered, businesses were established, factories were producing, schools and hospitals were opened, colleges were founded, and agricultural research was being conducted. The soil was good, the climate was favorable, religious freedom was wonderful, and there were many economic opportunities. Political non-interference provided the context in which all the above could combine to make life in Russia very good.

By 1914 seven percent of Russia's agricultural machinery was being produced in Mennonite factories. Much of her best wheat, for home use and for export, came from Mennonite farms. Many improved seed strains and mechanical innovations came from Mennonite research.

The Empress of Russia's offer was not exclusive to Mennonites. In fact, they made up only about 3% of all German people who took advantage of her generous offer. By the time of the Bolshevik Revolution, this total Germanic population, scattered in ethnic enclaves throughout Ukraine, southern Russia, and Asiatic Russia, numbered about two million persons, mostly Lutherans, but also Catholics and Baptists.

Most of these Germanic immigrants maintained their own culture, not blending well with the Slavic culture of the majority. Obviously, this considerable Germanic population was perceived as an unreliable threat when Russia became engaged in the Great War with Germany.

Trouble in Utopia

> *Then a new king, who did not know about Joseph, came to power in Egypt. "Look," he said to his people, "the Israelites have become much too numerous for us. Come, we must deal shrewdly with them, or they will become even more numerous and, if war breaks out, will join our enemies, fight against us and leave the country."* – Exodus 1:8-10 NIV

Nothing stays the same, and utopias don't last. Nationalism was on the rise in Russia as well. In an early step to unify and integrate these minority cultural groups, the government, in 1874, ordered the Russian language to be taught in the schools, and all able-bodied, young men were ordered to serve in the army. Thus, the most cherished promise which drew the Mennonites to Russia in the first place, was annulled.

The Mennonites responded by sending a delegation to investigate the possibility of moving to North America. They brought back a favorable report. Many of the Mennonites decided to emigrate again, this time to the pioneering frontiers of Kansas and Nebraska, in the USA, or the new Province of Manitoba, in Canada.

Most of them favored going to Canada instead of the United States because of the Canadian government's definite promise that they would never be drawn into military service. In all, about eighteen thousand Mennonites emigrated before the Russian government relented and permitted the young Mennonite men to do alternative service in the forests, under their own organization, instead of doing military service.

For another forty years, things went reasonably well for the Mennonites in Russia. They continued to prosper, while their indigenous neighbors remained in poverty. They contributed significantly to the development of agriculture and the economy of the Russian Empire. Yet they kept to themselves, separated from the Russian people and culture.

They were a foreign Germanic enclave, prospering amid a poor and backward society, which they looked down upon with sometimes obvious disdain. Theirs was an identity that later caused them much suffering, as Russia fought two wars against Germany in the first half of the twentieth century.

Amid prosperity, there were also inequalities and injustices that brought shame on the Mennonites. As their numbers multiplied, they could not all have land. Farms were fixed at 176 acres and could not be divided. So, the landless sons had to find jobs, join a trade, or migrate to a new settlement. Landless members had no civic or economic rights and were second class.

And while each settlement was surrounded with large tracts of surplus land, the landless were not allowed to have it, buy it, or rent it. These lands were usually rented to well-to-do farmers. Landless members were given a plot in the village, big enough for a house and a vegetable garden.

Some of the rich Mennonites even went outside of the settlements and bought large tracts of land to farm, some of them as large as twenty thousand acres.

By 1917, two thirds of the colonists were landless. They had to be laborers on the farms and in the factories of the wealthy. Some were very poor. And the Russian laborers were often treated worse.

When the Revolution put them in the position of power, many of those laborers, remembering the harshness and brutality with which they had been treated, came back for sweet and horrible revenge.

Revolution and the End of Utopia

The good times came to a final and brutal end with the defeat of Czarist Russia by Germany and the subsequent fall of the Imperial regime in the Revolution of 1917; and the following wars that took place, until the Bolsheviks established their absolute control by 1921. Those were times of social upheaval, revolution and counter-revolution, breakdown of law and order, and chaos. Marauding bands of anarchists, or just plain thieves, roamed about, murdering, and plundering unprotected villages.

Those were the years when people, who were used to the finer things of civilization, had to learn that "power comes out of the barrel of a gun"; that no matter how much one's intelligence, or how refined his character, or disciplined his life, or benevolent his conduct, or strong his influence in the community, he was no match for an idiot with a gun.

Those were times when people, who were used to being pampered or pampering themselves and their children, had to learn the agony of desperate and cruel hunger, of watching their children starve to death before their own eyes, and of being too weak to give them a proper burial.

2

Surviving a Revolution

In 1917, the nineteen-year-old Jacob Johann Friesen was far away from home working in Siberia's northern forests at Hierman Nyatchka. He was one of about 12,000 young Mennonite boys who, by reason of their non-resistant beliefs, were granted conscientious objector status and assigned alternative to military service under the Forestry Service Commission.

Because of their unpopular and unpatriotic stance, they were despised, and because they were of Germanic ethnic and cultural background, they were distrusted. They were contemptuously referred to as "bush monkeys."

Nineteen-year-old Jacob Friesen doing alternative to military service under the Forestry Service Commission in 1917

Jacob was a member of a company of fifty-six such young men. It had been six months since he had left home. It was for the first time—and he was homesick.

Then news of the overthrow of the Czarist Government, and the subsequent withdrawal of Russia from the war with Germany reached them. With law and order quickly breaking down, and the country falling into chaos, Jacob and his fellow forestry service workers joined the rush of soldiers, government workers, and many others to get home to their loved ones as quickly as possible. A group of eleven of them started out together. They passed Sverdlovsk in Ekaterinoslav in the Ural Mountains, where the deposed Tzar Nicholas II was later murdered in a cellar along with his Empress, a son, and four daughters on the night of July 16, 1918.

At Chelyabinsk Jacob was separated from most of his companions and tried to make it on his own. He didn't know how to get around on the railroad system. He had never seen a train before his journey to the North. He didn't always know where he was going nor the best way to get home. He asked directions from the railroad conductors. They advised him not to go to Moscow as there was a lot of shooting going on there including big cannon fire. Instead, he should go back east across the Ural Mountains.

He experienced a tale of horror. Thousands crowded to board the overloaded train. There was no food in Moscow, and people were struggling to get to Siberia where there was still food.

Soldiers were given first chance to board the train, so he bought a uniform from a second-hand clothing vendor and got on board. He had no money left, but with a soldier's uniform and a piece of paper with a blue stamp, one could ride most any place. It didn't always matter what the paper said or who's the signature, as most of the officials were illiterate, but the stamp was essential.

One of his buddies, Henry Penner came with five suitcases, some of them six feet long. He had to cross thirteen tracks to board the train. Rather than abandon his goods, he lost his chance to ride. He told Jacob, who had only a suitcase and a handbag, to go on ahead.

There was no room inside the train, so he and hundreds of others climbed on the roof. They tied themselves onto the ventilation chimneys. They were ordered not to lift their heads up. Then the overloaded train sped off to its destination.

They passed under low wires at a high speed. Anybody who failed to keep his head down got caught by the wires and was thrown off at sixty-five miles per hour. He counted sixteen men hanging from the wires. When they stopped, he noticed that the wheels of the train were splashed with the blood of those who fell.

As the train approached the Ural Mountains, Jacob remembered that his half-brother lived east of them in Slavgorod, Barnaul, in the Mennonite village of Shengwezie. So, he got off the train and found the home of his half-brother. After visiting them, he continued by train to Ufa, where the railroad makes many cuts through the Ural Mountains. At Ufa, he connected with another train going south to Samara (now Kuybychev) on the Volga, then east to Sorochinsk.

There he left the train and walked the fifty-five miles north to his home in Ischalka, a small Mennonite village in Samara Province. He had no money and no food, so he had to depend on the kindness of the people. He did not dare to talk German or let the Russian people know that he was German, or there would be no hospitality shown.

Finally, he came to a Russian village where his father, Johann Gerhard Friesen, was known. There he told the people who he was, and they took him in and fed him. He finally reached home eleven days after starting out. Henry Penner arrived at his home near Ufa five days later. Eventually, all fifty-six of the CO's arrived at their homes safely.

Jacob found that, the war being over, two of his half-brothers, Abraham, and Peter, had returned from the battle front in the south where they were doing non-combatant service in the army, that is, picking up the wounded and taking them to the army hospital.

He found that his father was not well, all the boys were coming home, winter was beginning, there was no work to earn something, and there was not much food at home either. His father sold a team of horses and bought flour, meat, and other necessities for the winter. The boys found part time work in a factory making blue alcohol for the army hospitals.

When the Russian neighbor boys came back from the war, they were old friends again. They would greet the German boys, "Hello, you returned!" Jacob says, "We couldn't tell them we weren't fighting." They would sit down together and drink tea and eat horse sausage and talk.

Later that winter Jacob got permission from his dad to take a team of horses and go to visit his friends from the forestry service in the other Mennonite villages. His father assumed he was going to look for a wife but let him go.

He arrived at a village thirty miles away the next evening. He got together with four of his friends. They brought some girls along. Jacob played the organ. Then he says, "We forgot we were Mennonites." The playing was good; they got on the happy side and began playing polkas.

Soon the old mother came out of her bedroom and rebuked them. So, they stopped the polka and sang some hymns and went to bed. The next day he went home.

In the spring he decided to marry a girl from his own village. But that fall, on September 16, 1918, his father died. This put a delay in his marriage plans (Extracted from the author's tape recording of Jacob Friesen's memories).

Jacob and Justina Start a Family

Another year passed before Jacob Johann Friesen and Justina Aaron Warkentin were married on November 30, 1919, in the little village of Ischalka in Samara, Russia. They were very poor. Both came from large poor families, and both had lost their fathers. Jacob had no land and no horses of his own.

At first, through that winter, the newlyweds lived in with his now widowed mother, Anna (Penner) Friesen. In the spring, they built their own house at the west end of the main street of the village. His mother had given them the land, and the couple built the house themselves.

They made sun dried bricks of clay and straw and laid them up and smeared them with a plaster of clay and cow dung mixed with straw. The result was then whitewashed. The roof was made with thin poles tied together and covered with straw or grass. It looked nice and was warm. The floor was also a smeared mix of clay and cow dung. The floor had to be re-smeared often, as the mix didn't hold up very well to foot traffic. This house was still standing there in 1956, when Justina's sister Maria Klassen visited the village.

Being the woman, Justina did most of the smearing herself, lugging big buckets of mud and water to the building site, and smearing it properly. She was determined to have the house ready so that her first child could be born in her own home.

She worked so hard that when the time came, the house was ready, but her health was bad. She had a very difficult delivery which almost cost her life. Her mother, Elisabet (Huebert) Warkentin, and a midwife, did all they could, prayed, and said: "We're in God's hands." God's hands were sufficient. Little Elizabeth Winnifred Friesen was born in her own home, healthy and normal in every way. God was with her from the beginning.

The first three of Jacob and Justina's children were born there in their first home. Elizabeth Winnifred was born on August 24, 1920. Her brother Jacob Peter, or." Jake," was born on February 10, 1922. Her baby sister, Aganetha (Neta) Valentine, was born on February 14, 1924.

Ancestry

Jacob Friesen's family roots can be traced back to the village of Waldick, Friesland, near the Holland border, where his grandfather, Gerhard Friesen, was born in 1810. He was carried as a baby by his parents from Waldick directly to Gebiet Kherson (also "Cherson"), Crimea, in 1812. His parents' names we do not know. Gerhard married Aganetha Janzen, probably in the Molotschna colony. Aganetha, Jacob's grandmother, was born on August 21, 1832, in Molotschna, Crimea, Ukraine, to Johann Jacob F Janzen and Katharina D K Friesen. Gerhard and Aganetha had one son, Johann Gerhard Friesen, born on March 28, 1857.

Aganetha died in 1877, aged about forty-five in Molotschna. Some of her roots can be traced all the way back to Jacob's five-times-great-grandparents, Isaac Claassen, born on March 14, 1670, and Margaretha Bergmann, born on October 13, 1667.

In 1892, at eighty-two years of age, Gerhard moved to Ischalka with his son, Johann Gerhard Friesen, and his family, along with a brother, whose name has been lost. Ischalka was a village in the new Pleschanow colony in New Samara in the Volga region. Gerhard was photographed at Ischalka in 1907 when he was ninety-seven years old. His birth and death dates we do not know.

The Friesen homestead in Ischalka, Samara, Russia in 1907. Sitting on the chair is Jacob's ninety-seven-year-old grandfather, Gerhard Friesen. Standing in the lefthand corner is his father, Johann Gerhard Friesen, and beside him is Jacob's mother, Anna, holding baby Isbrand. Dietrich standing beside her. In front of Gerhard, left to right are Peter, Isaac,

Johann sitting on the reaper, Kornelius, Anna, Lena, and Tina. On the wagon are two Russian workers. The boys, Heinrich, Abraham, and Jacob are behind them. (In those days and in their setting, very few photos were taken, and in the family's troubled pilgrimage, even fewer photos survived.)

Gerhard's son, Johann Gerhard Friesen, was born at Petershagen, Molotschna, Ukraine. He was married on Feb. 22, 1881, to Helena Wiens who was born March 24, 1861, at Orloff, and baptized in Karassan, Crimea, on Pentecost, 1880. To them were born six children in nine years. But only three lived to maturity. Helena died on May 30, 1890, two and one-half months after her last baby was born. The baby died three months later.

Johann, having three small children to raise, very quickly married again. This time he married Anna David Penner out of Sparau. Being of a later migration, she was born in Poland on March 28, 1865. She was baptized in Karassan in 1886 by Elder Abram Friesen.

To them were born twelve children in sixteen years. Eight sons and one daughter reached maturity. Their firstborn, Peter was born in the Crimea on June 23, 1891, one year and twenty-three days after Johann's first wife died. Anna gave birth again on August 1st of 1892, the year the family moved with Johann's eighty-two-year-old father to Ischalka, New Samara. Whether Isaac was born in Crimea or Ischalka, we do not know.

Their third son, Heinrich, died as a non-combatant on the war front in Austria on May 6, 1916, after being sick of typhus for fourteen days.

Being the fifth son of the second marriage, Jacob Johann Friesen, was born in Ischalka on October 25, 1898. His father, Johann, died on September 16, 1918, at the age of sixty-one years. His mother, Anna, died on March 29, 1937, at seventy-two years of age. [From notes collected from Lena Friesen and notes kept by Liese Barkman written by Katherine Schmidt's son. "*Ausgewandert bei Katharine II nach Ukraina, Gebiet Cherson. Wir stammen von Friesland, Hollandishe Grenze. Dorf Waldick, Kreis Meimrich (Memcik).*" Translated: "Emigrated by Katherine II to Ukraine Gebiet Kherson. Our ancestry is from Friesland - Holland border village Waldick Kries Meimrich Memcik."]

An interesting anecdote concerning their sixth son, Kornelius Friesen, born on April 14, 1900. He was not a healthy person, had heart problems.

His doctor advised him not to marry and to limit his work. He was a devout Christian and read his Bible a lot and spent much time in prayer.

One Sunday morning in May 1940, at breakfast, he requested everyone to be home that evening at nine o'clock p.m. because he was going to die at that time. An angel had told him that night to prepare himself because he was going to die. The family took this prophesy lightly but were there in the evening. He was sitting in a chair at nine o'clock when he slumped over dead. It was a stirring experience for the family. He was forty years old and unmarried. [Helen Friesen Heide reported this to Elizabeth in July 1980.]

Justina Aaron Warkentin, was born at Herzenberg, Ekaterinoslav Province, Ukraine, on September 22nd, 1896. Justina was the second daughter and fourth child of Aaron A. Warkentin and Elisabet Huebert. Aaron was the fifth of a long line of Aaron A. Warkentins. He was born on June 28, 1869. The Warkentins moved to New Samara and owned one of the better farms in Ischalka. Aaron loved horses and drove the liveliest team in the village. He was no singer, but when alone, he could sing the whole songbook through. A neighbor said, "He was a saved person." He had seen him praying out behind a back shed.

Aaron Warkentin was killed in an accident on June 3, 1905, at age thirty-six, when Justina was nine. He was hauling a load of logs by horse and wagon downhill when he slipped and fell forward, and the wagon went over him and crushed his chest. Justina would stand by the window when it was raining and cry and cry. Her daddy was getting wet in the graveyard.

Justina's paternal grandfather was also Aaron A. Warkentin. He was married to Maria Born. He had a genealogical history written in Dutch tracing their ancestry back to their migration directly from The Netherlands to Russia. When Justina was a teenager, her grandfather advised her to copy it, but she didn't understand Dutch and didn't see the importance of it, so it was lost.

Justina's mother, Elisabet Huebert, was born on September 16, 1871, to Nikolai Huebert and Elisabet Neuman. She bore eight children to Aaron. Six of them reached maturity. She suffered much from asthma and bronchitis. She died on February 22, 1938, at the age of sixty-seven years.

Justina's mother and siblings, John, Nikolai, and Maria Warkentin (Photo taken in Russia in 1924 and sent to family in Canada)

Jacob Friesen's mother, Anna in Ischalka, in 1924 with her then single children, standing left to right, Isbrand, Dietrich and Abram; sitting: Kornelius, Mother Anna, and Anna. (Photo taken in Russia in 1924 and sent to family in Canada)

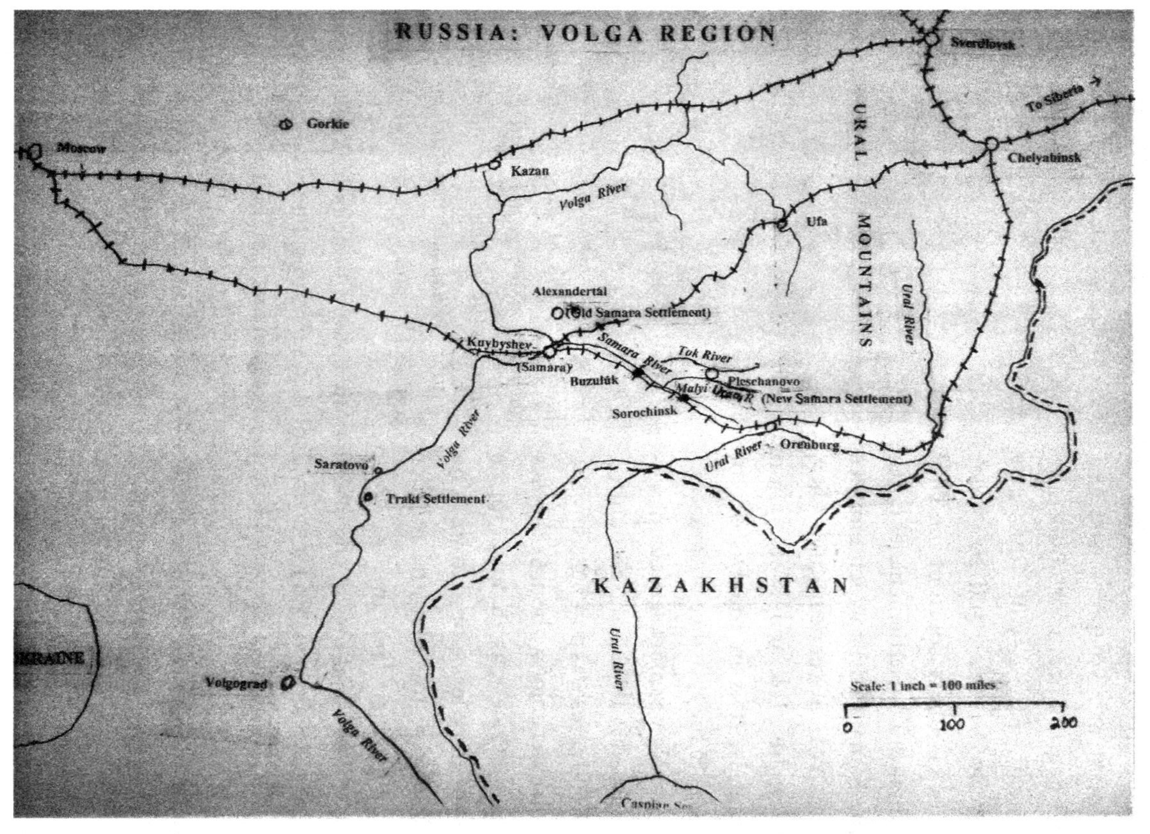

Sketch of the location of the New Samara Settlement in respect to the larger Volga Region of Russia in which it was located

Ischalka

Ischalka was one of a group of fourteen Mennonite villages in the New Samara or Pleschanow settlement at 53 degrees east and 52.55 degrees north, or about 200 miles east of the city of Kuybyshev (formerly "Samara") and 200 miles west of Orenburg south of the Ural Mountains. This settlement lies north of the Samara River which empties into the Volga River near Kuybyshev, between its Tok and Malyi Uran tributaries. It is in the District of Busuluk in the Province of Samara.

Jacob Friesen's mother, Anna, sitting with his sister, Anna, and brothers Nicholas (tallest) and Isbrand standing behind – (Photo taken in Russia in 1938 and sent to family in Canada)

The New Samara settlement was established in 1890. Land amounting to 59,400 acres was purchased by the Molotschna colony, about 900 miles to the southwest, as an outlet for its growing landless population. The settlers were to repay the mother colony for their land in time. The other villages making up the Pleschanow colony, besides Ischalka, were Ahrenskol, Kamensk, Bogomasow, Dolinsk, Donskoje, Podolsk, Lugowsk, Jugowka, Klinok, Krassikowo, Kuterija, Kaltan, and Jasoikino.

Land for Ischalka was purchased from the Russian village of Nowo-Nickoljsk. The settlers built the village with twenty-one farmsteads of thirty, forty, fifty, and even one hundred acres and two outlying farms of 500 acres together. One of these belonged to Aaron Warkentin and the other to Johan and Benjamin Voth, both well-to-do and relatives of Justina. The first mayor was Jacob J. Stobbe, then David Regehr, and then Johan Willms.

A school was built in 1899 and the first teachers were Peter Duerksen, D. Goertzen, David Regehr, and Julius Plett. Peter J. Stobbe, the first preacher, held services each Sunday in the schoolhouse. In 1912 Nicholai Johan Friesen moved to Ischalka and served as minister and teacher for many years. He was from Molotschna and was a trained teacher. Heinrich Willems and a certain Mr. Schmitt were choir leaders. There was choir practice three times per week.

For major celebrations such as Pentecost, baptism, and communion, the worshipers went to the big church in Pleschanow.

The village also had a mill. In 1926, thirty-eight families or 212 people lived in Ischalka. They lived on twenty-two farms and farmed 2,700 acres. Ischalka was a very poor village and was spared some of the worst suffering from marauding bandits and anarchists that the richer villages endured during the turbulent years following the revolution.

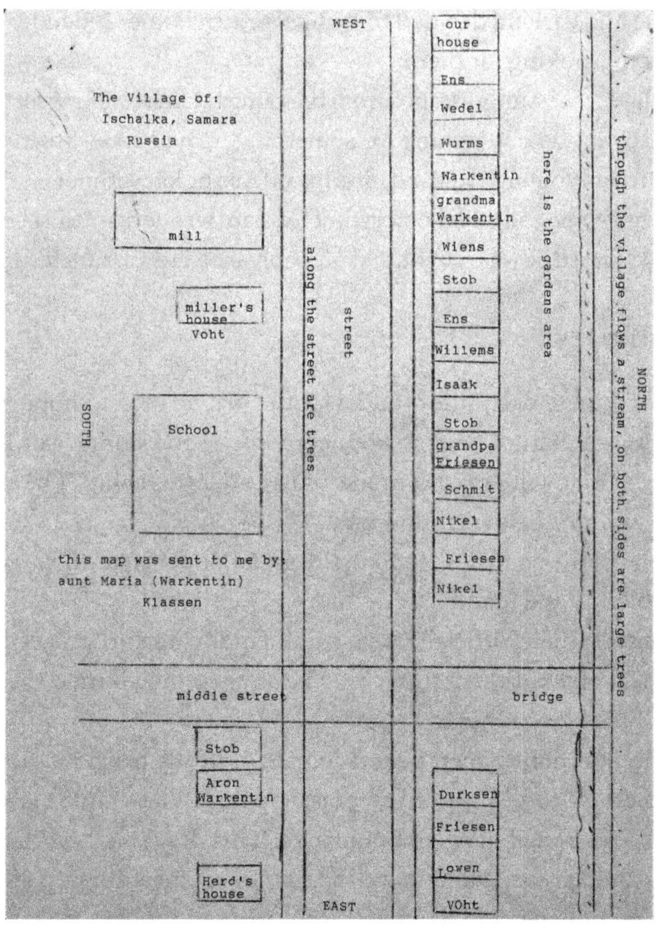

A layout of the Village of Ischalka drawn by Elizabeth (Friesen) Hansen as remembered by her mother, Justina Friesen, the way they left it in 1924

Terror

Those were hard times for everybody in Russia, and the young Friesen family endured their share of suffering. There was hunger and terror. Different armies came and went, taking horses and cattle and food stocks, including seed grains. Marauding bands of bandits came and took what was left. Without the cattle, there was not enough milk or meat. Without the work horses, it was impossible to plow enough land to produce the food that was needed. The economic structures collapsed, and it became difficult to buy food.

A neighbor was shot through the head while trying to flee on horseback.

One of Justina's brothers, Gerhard Warkentin was away in the Forestry service. He and a friend decided to escape, return home, and hide when the officials came looking for them.

They had successfully escaped from the camp but were waiting for transport home. Gerhard was out looking for something, maybe food, when the train came. His friend couldn't wait and miss his ride, so he left without Gerhard. His friend arrived home and told the story, but Gerhard was never seen or heard from again. It is assumed he was caught, and probably shot. He was nineteen years old.

Grasshoppers

On top of all these calamities there was the plague of grasshoppers which lasted for three years. The grasshoppers came in the summer of 1920 and returned the following two summers. They ate everything. They even ate the onions an inch below ground level.

Of course, the chickens ate so many grasshoppers that their eggs stank and were bloody and inedible.

The government officials ordered all landowners to go out and pick grasshoppers and put them in sacks. The women then buried the sacks in trenches. This didn't seem to help.

So, the Mennonite men persuaded the officials to allow them to try a better method to get rid of the grasshoppers. They built more than a hundred horse-drawn drags out of planks. This drag was designed so that a person would sit on it and drive the horses, as they dragged it over the ground, crushing the grasshoppers.

On a given day, early in the morning while the grasshoppers were still on the ground, all the farmers went out in their fields with their horses and these drags. They dragged them around and around until they scrapped all the land, killing millions of grasshoppers.

But the more they crushed them, the more the grasshoppers multiplied. Apparently, as the drags crushed the grasshoppers, they also buried the eggs in the soil where they soon hatched into more grasshoppers.

Finally, the farmers gave up, and the Russian officials agreed that there was nothing more they could do. Only God could save them from this plague. The Christians prayed. Then in August of 1922 clouds came up. A terrible rain and hailstorm followed which washed the land clean. After that there were no more grasshoppers. (Extracted from Jacob Friesen's tape-recorded memories in the author's possession).

Famine

The unreasonable requisitioning of livestock and farm products by the various passing armies and marauding bands, and the plague of grasshoppers, combined with the extended drought of 1920 - 21 to make a widespread famine of tragic proportions. The famine reached its worst in 1921 and 1922. Cornelius F. Klassen made a trip through the settlements in December of 1921 to arrange for American Mennonite Relief. He found that there was no bread left in the Volga region. His biographer reported:

> *In the Samara Guberniya (state) he found nothing but famine and death. Many villages were deserted, their thatched roofs torn off in an attempt to keep livestock alive.... Some people had tried to flee the villages but had died along the roadsides. Many were forced to eat tree bark, straw and various wild animals like rats, gophers, and crows or even domestic pets like cats and dogs. The starving hordes would beg from house to house crying for "bread in God's name!"* (Klassen, p.52).

The village of Ischalka got some relief, as Nicholas N. Friesen recalls in correspondence with Elizabeth from his home in British Columbia:

> *We were plagued by grasshoppers in 1921. Whether it was the "volosts" or the churches who helped out I do not know, but father (Nikolai Friesen, the minister in Ischalka) and*

his brother-in-law Jakob Stobbe went to Siberia, where the harvest was plentiful, to obtain wheat. They returned with three railroad cars full of grain.

At this time, we had no stable government with little or no communication. While away, Father contracted typhoid fever. He was ill for more than three months and meanwhile we starved a home. How delicious was the first slice of bread we enjoyed after his return! I still think it sinful to waste precious food.

Baby Jacob Peter, or "Jake", was born into the Friesen home on February 10, 1922. He soon had a starvation belly. Yet he learned to walk at nine months. Justina talked of surviving for months on a diet of potatoes only, until spring brought new growth. It hurt so deeply not to be able to give your children something to eat.

Sometimes Jacob would go out to the fields to trap gophers to feed his family. Little Elizabeth would play with those he caught and then cry when he took them away to dress them. One day his unmarried brother came by and begged to borrow one gopher until he could catch some because he was very hungry. He took that gopher and walked away eating it raw and finished it before reaching his house which was just a short distance down the street.

One day Justina saw a Russian man they knew out digging by himself. They went out to him and found him trying to bury his wife who had died of starvation. Someone else had offered to care for the man's child, but it was so starved that they over fed it, and it also died.

Some people took advantage of the hardships of others. The family traded for or bought a bag of beets. On the top they were good, but further down in the bag they were poorer, and, in the bottom, there was just dirt.

Relief

It was in answer to the cries and prayers of these desperate people, that God moved the hearts of North American Mennonites to organize a "Mennonite Central Committee" (MCC) in 1920, to send food shipments from more than 6,000 miles away, to relieve the hunger of their brothers and sister in Russia in 1921-23. And God moved the hearts of thousands of Christ followers to pour out a torrent of generosity, contributing food and clothing and other relief goods that saved the lives of thousands of starving Mennonites and other Russians.

And it saved the lives of the Jacob Friesen family, including the little girl, Elizabeth, who was to become my mother. MCC also negotiated with the Canadian Department of Immigration, the Canadian Pacific Railroad (CPR) and the Government of Russia to arrange for those Mennonites who wished, and were qualified, to immigrate to Canada.

The first relief food to reach Russia was distributed in New Samara in mid-December 1921. The village elders chose someone to distribute this food. There was much discontent and suspicion about the fairness of the distribution. Some hoarded while their neighbors starved. One man boasted, "See how my children are blooming!" The neighbor replied, "Mine have about finished blooming."

MCC also sent fifty Fordson tractors and plows and seed to the Volga region to help them get started again, as the horses were mostly gone. Those tractors plowed 17,500 acres of land the following year, between five to ten acres per family.

Others demonstrated the spirit of Christ in sharing the little they had with those less fortunate. A certain neighbor lady would save a little bit of her food and bring it over for little Elizabeth and would sit and watch her eat it all and marvel how she picked up every speck and crumb.

Elizabeth recalls from her childhood memories:

> *Another time I came to Grandma's and there was a man at the door asking for something to eat. Grandma told Aunt Maria to "Give him a chunk of bread!" She gave him a chunk of bread and he sat right there on the step outside the door eating this bread and I stood there watching. When he was done, he got up and left. This is the only vision, in memory, that I have of that grandmother, "Give him a chunk of bread!"*

From a Child's Viewpoint

Elizabeth writes of some of her earliest impressions:

> *I was four years old when we left Russia. There was a neighbor girl that came and played with me quite a bit. One day we*

decided to run away. Living at the end of the village we started out into the prairie. I don't know how far we went. I still remember how the ground looked, like our prairie. Ahead there were some bushes and we saw something moving, it looked like it was running back and forth, we stopped. What was it? We decided it was wolves and ran back home as fast as we could. I don't remember ever running away from home again. Later in life, remembering what it looked like, I decided it was heat waves against the clump of trees....

I remember, one evening Mom and Dad were working in the garden and I was running around. There was an anthill and Mom warned me not to get too close. But being either too curious or too careless I ran right into it. The ants lost no time climbing up my legs. I hollered and screamed, jumping up and down. Mom came running, "I told you to keep away from there!" she scolded as she brushed the ants off and took me to the house.

In summer it was customary for everyone to take a nap after dinner. Their day started very early, and they worked hard so in the heat of the day was rest time. The village was quietly resting, my parents included, and I thought it was a good time to visit Grandma. Mother's family lived closer than Dad's and they were well beloved. There was Aunt Maria, Mom's only sister, and she loved us dearly. So, nothing like sneaking a visit. I came there, the door was latched, and everyone sleeping. I was prepared to wait, but the neighbor's dog decided to run through the fruit bushes in Grandma's garden right then. I was so frightened, I hollered and screamed pounding on the door.

Aunt Maria came to the door all sleepy and disturbed looking, "You will wake Grandma.", she scolded. "The dog, the dog!" was all I could sob. "The dog won't hurt you!", she consoled. She took me in and made me sit on a chair till they were finished their nap. That was a bit disappointing. I used to sneak off to Grandma's quite often. If Mom found me missing, she'd find me there. I couldn't seem to be trained not to. (Elizabeth Hansen, Unpublished manuscript, 1990, pp. 2, 3)

3

Searching Further

Leave your country, your people and your father's household and go to the land I will show you. I will make you into a great nation and I will bless you; I will make your name great, and you will be a blessing. – Genesis 12:1-2 NIV

Immigration in the Air

It was during those hard times that the Mennonite Central Committee negotiated with the Canadian Department of Immigration, the Canadian Pacific Railroad (CPR), and the Russian Government to arrange for the Mennonites to emigrate to Canada. The CPR arranged the transportation and took care of screening the applicants to meet the Canadian Government's immigration requirements. The CPR sent Dr. Drury from Canada to the Mennonite villages to interview and inspect the applicants. Those with communicable diseases were rejected.

There were two categories of emigrants: Those who paid cash, and those who were given passage on credit upon their agreeing to pay principle plus interest within a year of reaching Canada. The costs of passage were seventy-five dollars for adults and fifty dollars for children. The Canadian Mennonite Board of Colonization was formed to act as guarantor for the loan and would organize for their reception in Canada.

Jacob Friesen wanted his family to emigrate. As Lenin had just died, he expected that the incoming leadership of Russia would likely pass to Joseph Stalin. He had followed Stalin's rise in the Communist party and was concerned about what the future for him and his family would be if they stayed in Russia under Stalin. So, he thought it best to emigrate to Canada, but doubted he would be accepted because he had malaria. He told his wife to go on alone if he was rejected.

However, he found that Canadians would take malaria patients, "even if they were on a stretcher." Dr. Drury gave him a prescription for the Red Cross to give him quinine at Kuybyshev.

Their parents decided to stay. Justina's sister Maria wanted to go but was not allowed because she had trachoma. Her brother Johann decided to go. Jacob's younger brother Dietrich wanted to go but his older brothers would not sign for him. Years later in corresponding to his friend, Johann, Dietrich would address him, "O you lucky one!"

Justina's oldest brother Aaron was cleared to go, but his wife was sick and couldn't go. Elizabeth writes:

> *He could not walk out on his sick wife, though he was urged by some to do so. She died later but by then the doors were closed and he couldn't come. This uncle was a carpenter and had made me a crib and highchair. It was all left behind. Mom gave most everything away, her Bible and songbook to her sister and any other precious thing she had, partly because her sister was so inconsolable, and Mom felt so bad she couldn't come.*
>
> *Years later, Aunt Maria wrote they had just one old song book with the pages falling out, and Mother wondered if it was the one, she had given her* (p. 4).

The family was preparing to leave in late summer of 1924. Elizabeth recalls:

> *I remember the potatoes. Our parents had sold them to some Russians. One day we children were having our noonday nap, Mother and Dad were gone (Sometimes I say I've been a babysitter since I was four years old). I was awakened by some people talking outside the window. I saw shadows moving across the walls and ceiling and was frightened.... The people*

> *moved closer to the window, and I heard and understood what they were saying (So I understood Russian at age four). They had come for the potatoes. I relaxed and went back to sleep* (p. 3).

The life of an immigrant is never easy, and parting from family and friends and favorite possessions, and saying goodbye to all one has ever known and held dear, is the hardest part. Again, Elizabeth shares what she remembers as a child:

> *It is strange I cannot remember taking leave of Mother's side of the house. They were my favorites, my favorite grandma, my favorite aunt, I was there every chance I had or could take but I can't remember the leave taking. This I remember... on Dad's side of the house, we were in the wagon ready to leave, and Grandma Friesen was standing by the wagon begging, coaxing me to stay, and I reached my hands out to her and Mom pulled me back.*
>
> *They tell me, when we were getting ready to leave, I followed Aunt Maria around and said, "It is so bad for me in 'Merica." ... I don't remember a thing of our trip by wagon and then by train to Riga.* (p. 4).

Farewell to Russia!

The community had a farewell service for those who were emigrating on Sunday, October 19, 1924. One of the songs they sang was "Take Thou My Hand O Father and Lead Thou Me" (So Nimm Denn Meine Hande).

1. *Take Thou my hand O Father, and lead Thou me,*
   Until my journey endeth, eternally.
   Alone I will not wander One single day;
   Be Thou my true companion and with me stay.

2. *O cover with Thy mercy My poor weak heart!*
   Let every thought rebellious From me depart.
   Permit Thy child to linger Here at Thy feet,

And blindly trust Thy goodness With faith complete.

3. *Though naught of Thy great power May move my soul,*
With Thee thru night and darkness I reach the goal.
Take then my hands, O Father, and lead Thou me,
Until my journey endeth, eternally.

Julie Katharina Haussmann, 1862, Tr. H. Brueckner, 1942

Jacob and Justina Friesen and their three small children left their home in Ischalka forever on October 20, 1924. Baby Aganetha (Neta) Valentine had joined the family on February 14th. They travelled with other emigrants by horse and wagon to the railroad station at Sorochinsk fifty-five miles away.

On Tuesday, October 21, they boarded a train for Moscow. In Moscow they stayed at the Immigration Hotel until their documents were processed, fares arranged, and further medical checks were done. In all about 22,000 Mennonite emigrants passed through this hotel from 1923 to 1929. From there they linked up with an emigrant train taking many others like themselves to the port city of Riga in Latvia.

They stopped in Russia for the last time at the border town of Ceberch at the "Red Gate." Everybody was extremely tense as the uniformed customs officers boarded the train for a final checking. They were known to be ruthless in pulling people off the train without cause or on the smallest pretext, or to confiscate any last family treasure or keepsake that they might desire. A lot of silent prayers went up as the officers checked everyone carefully.

Then the engine was unhooked, and a Latvian locomotive took its place. The crew was replaced with a Latvian crew. A Red Army military band stood by and sang "The International" as a farewell song, as the train slowly crossed the Russian border into Latvia. As soon as the train crossed the line, the emigrants all joined their hearts and voices in a mighty chorus singing "Grosser Gott Wir Loben Dich" ("Holy God, We Praise Thy Name!"). It was an indescribable emotional moment of relief and gratitude.

Holy God, we praise Thy name.
Lord of all, we bow before Thee,
All on earth Thy scepter claim,

All in heav'n above adore Thee.
Infinite Thy vast domain,
Everlasting is Thy reign.

Hark the loud celestial hymn,
Angel choirs above are raising.
Cherubim and Seraphim,
In unceasing chorus praising,
Fill the heav'ns with sweet accord:
Holy, Holy, Holy Lord.

Lo! The apostolic train
Joins Thy sacred name to hallow.
Prophets swell the glad refrain,
And the white-robed martyrs follow.
And from morn to set of sun,
Through the Church the song goes on.

Holy Father, Holy Son,
Holy Spirit, Three we name Thee.
While in essence only One,
Undivided God, we claim Thee,
And adoring bend the knee,
While we sing our praise to Thee.

– Late 4th century hymn, "Te Deum Laudamus",
Tr. Clarence Walworth, 1853

Breathing Freedom in Strange Lands

The train reached Rezekne, about thirty miles inside Latvia, on October 28, and reached Riga shortly after. At Riga they were welcomed at an Air Force base where they were given food and clean bedding. They were required to go through a rigid delousing and cleansing process before they were taken by train to the harbor city of Libau where they boarded the "Baltara," a ship of the United Baltic Corp. Ltd., on November 1st. The ship crossed the Baltic Sea and went through the Kiel Canal into the North Sea.

Jacob Friesen was very impressed with the Kiel Canal. At first the passengers were horrified as the ship seemed to be sailing right into bridges that crossed the canal. Each time they were sure there was going to be a horrible accident. But just when the spectators braced themselves for the impact, the bridge just automatically swung aside or raised up in the nick of time. The emigrants were amazed. It was also their first time to see real coal.

In the North Sea they ran into a violent storm. Jacob remembers that he was the only passenger along with only five stewards that didn't get sick. Elizabeth remembers being on the ship:

> *We kids must not have gotten seasick. We ran all over. The cook gave us cookies, so he was our friend, we'd sit by the door waiting. The others got sick. I remember Uncle John being sick coming down a flight of stairs. I was down lower looking up and seeing him get sick. I ran off to tell Mom. Mom must have spent most of her time in bed. I remember being on deck with Dad* (p. 4).

The ship arrived in London on November 5th. It was the first time for the emigrants to see the effects of the tide. They stopped at London Bridge when the tide was out and waited eight hours for it to come in, so they could continue to the dock.

The ship was bumped by a big one that did some damage to it. There were about 2000 passengers on the ship. Many ran to that side to see what happened. So, the ship started to list on its side. The Captain quickly ordered them all to the other side and the ship straightened up. A major catastrophe was narrowly avoided.

The emigrants didn't see much of London, though Jacob was quite fearful of the double decker buses. He was sure they would tip.

Jacob had no decent clothes and no money. Ever the extrovert, he was happy to meet a group of German speaking Jews with whom he could talk. They observed that he had no clothes for the winter weather. He replied: "Yes, but my heart is still beating, and I'm so glad to get out alive!" One of the Jews gave him a good jacket. But he still had no good pants.

From London, five hundred emigrants took a train to Southampton. They went through the countryside at ninety miles per hour (from Jacob Friesen's recorded memories). They stayed in Southampton for four days where they again had to undergo a more rigorous cleansing and delousing process. Elizabeth describes it:

> *We were put in a large building and searched for lice and diseases.... We were thoroughly cleansed and purified by the British.... They combed the women's hair looking for lice and nits.... The women sat on chairs while the English ladies combed their hair with aluminum combs... and scissors. Any time they thought there was a louse or nit, they snipped a chunk of hair out. They were not gentle.... Mom told me how it hurt and how she cried and the lady doing it would look at her and pat her cheek. There were many tears shed that day. The British did not like immigrants. A few of the husbands saw how it was going, and before it was their wives turn, they said, "They are not going to treat you like that!", and they cut their wives hair right off to the skin. My parents cut my hair off too, but I guess Mother didn't have the courage... and went through the torture. Being a meek and submissive person, she didn't suffer quite as much as those who resisted. Some rebelled and got tortured for hours and even slapped.*
>
> *When they were done with the hair business, we had to strip and were herded into large showers. Mothers and their children into one large shower. My first shower. We were so frightened.... We got thoroughly washed* (p. 5).

This delousing and cleansing process was standard procedure for the immigration department, but it was very humiliating and traumatic for the Mennonite women who always prided themselves in their cleanliness and their modesty.

Some of the women managed to get their aluminum combs and brought them along as souvenirs. Elizabeth says, "If you don't know the significance of an aluminum comb try one when you have the chance.... try combing your long hair with an aluminum comb? It's an experience and doubly so if someone else does it."

When all the procedures were completed, the emigrants were allowed to board the S.S. Empress Of Scotland, a 25,160-ton ship for the trans-Atlantic voyage on November 8th.

This was a German passenger liner that was built in 1905 and was named "Kaiserin Augusta Victoria" At the time of building, it was the largest luxury liner in the world. It was 677 feet long and seventy-seven feet wide. It had four masts and two funnels and travelled at fifteen knots.

After being seized by the Allies, as a part of war reparations from defeated Germany, it was acquired by the Canadian Pacific Line in 1922 and re-outfitted and converted from coal to an oil burner. It had room for 459 first class, 478 second class, and 536 third class passengers, and took 500 crew members to service them and run the ship. It ran a regular service between Hamburg, Germany and Quebec city via Southampton and Cherbourg.

Anna Reimer Dyck writes of this trip in her book, *Anna, From the Caucasus to Canada,* translated and edited by Peter J. Klassen:

> *The emigrants crossed the Atlantic in the Empress of Scotland. By now it was November, and the trip was very stormy. Very often the passengers had to remain in their cabins, for the high winds drove the waves over the deck. One girl died on the voyage, and after ... a short burial address, her body was lowered into its watery grave. All the other passengers arrived safely in Quebec on November 16, 1924* (p. 86).

Justina told her children of seeing icebergs and bad storms, but she said the ship was not as rough as the first one because it was a lot bigger and more comfortable. Yet many were sick for the whole journey. When the shipload of immigrants landed in Quebec, they sang praises to God. It was a moving experience. The Canadians were impressed.

Pilgrims Land on Canadian Soil

At Quebec, they had to undergo another final health inspection. The CPR had arranged for the immigrants to be transported by train to Saskatchewan. It was an uncomfortable four-day ride, in the cold over-crowded train to Rosthern, where the Friesen family disembarked with others.

Now they were in Canada, strangers in a strange land, among a strange people with a strange language and strange customs. But they were met at the railroad station by Mennonites who had come before, their own kind of people to comfort them, welcome them, and help them make the adjustments to this new land.

Daniel Bueckert described an earlier arrival of immigrants at Rosthern in 1923:

> *When the first train of immigrants arrived in Rosthern in 1923 the receiving committee ordered the train to park a good distance beyond the station, because there were so many people at the station that they would have spilled on to the tracks. When the new passengers did detrain on the grass between the high elevators, a spontaneous chorus of "Nun Danket Alle Gott" almost like an explosion spread over the station area* (A private letter to Elizabeth Hansen).

Now thank we all our God
With heart and hands and voices,
Who wondrous things hath done,
In whom His world rejoices.
Who, from our mother's arms,
Hath blessed us on our way
With countless gifts of love,
And still is ours today.

O may this bounteous God
Through all our life be near us,
With ever joyful hearts
And blessed peace to cheer us.
And keep us in His grace,
And guide us when perplexed,
And free us from all ills
In this world and the next.

All praise and thanks to God,
The Father, now be given,
The Son, and Him who reigns
With them in highest heaven,

The one eternal God,
Whom earth and heav'n adore.
For thus it was, is now,
And shall be evermore. Amen

– Martin Rinckart, 1636, (Nun Danket Alle Gott) Tr. Cathern Winkworth, 1858

Searching for a Home

The immigrants were welcomed to find shelter in a church, until they could all be placed with families for the winter. That was no small undertaking for the poor Mennonite community, as they themselves were recent immigrants, and this train brought four hundred new people for their small houses to accommodate.

The Jacob Friesen family was taken in by the Bernhard Friesen family (no relative) in Eigenheim that first winter. Jacob helped him with his chores. They were given some clothing from a clothing department organized for that purpose. Elizabeth remembers:

> *The house was new and still unfinished, ... the bare two by fours were sticking out in one room.... One morning we found out a horse had died. We all had to go out to see it. It was laying there beside the barn. We felt so sad, stood, and mourned for a while. It was cold and snowing.*
>
> *One day they were sawing wood... and Mr. Friesen's brother got his hand cut. I remember them bringing him in and he was laying on the couch while they got ready to take him to the doctor* (p.6).

Tena Friesen, recounts a story her parents told in her unpublished Memoirs (a copy of which she gave to me):

> *My father had nothing warm to wear and it was bitter cold outside. The first time he ventured outside it was so cold he thought that he would freeze. A neighbor met him. This man gave my father a large heavy buffalo coat that I remember him wearing as late as 1938. He wore a thick fur cap with four*

> *flaps that could be either turned up or down depending on the weather. It was a very warm cap and I often wished that I could have one the same. My father looked awesome in his huge coat and large felt boots* (p.15).

Those immigrants had to discover the economic opportunities for themselves in this new land. Of course, it took some time for this to happen, and they tended to move around a lot during those first few years. There was such a heavy concentration of immigrants around Rosthern that jobs were scarce, and wages were extremely low.

At first, the family lived in the Mennonite community at Eigenheim near Rosthern. Jacob got a job in late winter working for Frank Henschel for ten dollars per month. But he got sick after two weeks and quit.

In early spring of 1925, Jacob moved his family to Hague, Saskatchewan. He left home to explore opportunities and to work wherever he could find it. Elizabeth recalls:

> *We lived in town in a large building, seemed it was a long one. We had our own rooms. There were other people living in there to. I remember one old gentleman. Easter morning Mom had hidden Easter eggs for us. There was a long hall, and we ran there looking for our eggs. This old gentleman came out of his room, I guess, to enjoy it with us. That is the first Easter egg hunt I remember* (p. 6).

Then Jacob found a job up in a bushy place along the North Saskatchewan River about thirty-five miles from Rosthern. A Ukrainian/Canadian farmer gave him thirty-five dollars per month for seeding. He also gave him a homesteader's house and a cow for milk. Kind neighbors gave them some chickens. Elizabeth recalls some events from that place:

> *For a while we lived in the bush, at least one summer, and Dad worked for a Russian. Once we were invited for supper. I think I'll never forget that home. It seems in the middle of the room hung this hammock where they kept the baby. Mom said that's the way they did in Russia, no draft on the baby. I also remember a baby swing made of spools, a board and string.*

The man was a noisy jovial boss. When he came in for supper, he washed noisily, splashing water over his face, and exhaling noisily at the same time. I stood and stared. I'd never seen the like! When we were seated around the table, he inhaled his drink with gusto! It left a lasting impression on me. I think I did more gawking than eating.

We had a house there in the bush and a cow. At milking time Mom would go out and call, "Babe - soo - hoo" and the cow would come. She saved cream for butter. This time she kept the cream in the churn. When she got the churn out to make butter it was thick with drowned mice. Just thick! You can't imagine! We had to dump it all. That was so disappointing.

One evening we kids were chopping wood, guess we were "helping" mother when I got my leg chopped with the axe, right on the shin. What agony! How I hollered! Mom came running and helped me to bed and took good care of me. Seems I spent some time in bed over that. The scar is still visible (pp. 7, 8).

(Back in Imperial Russia, the Mennonites didn't make a big distinction between "Ukrainians" and "Russians." If the person was not a Mennonite, he/she was assumed to be a "Russian" in their minds.)

After that the family moved near some Old Colony Mennonites. It must have been at Reinfeldt about one and one-half miles from Hague. Jacob was off working somewhere again. Elizabeth remembers some incidents from that place:

We lived among Old Colony people. Going past our house was a sandy road and we kids would play in the sand. One old gentleman came driving along one day having his nap as he drove. Neta was playing in the road, the horse sidestepped her, but the buggy went over her. The bump woke the old man, and he came carrying the limp child to its mother with much dismay and apologies. There was no apparent harm to the child, she came to again and all was well....

In one place we lived close by a school and some kids came and got us for their school picnic, our first school picnic and

> *our first ice cream that I remember. We also got acquainted with our first saskatoons. Mom was so thrilled over these nice berries. I don't know how thrilled she was when we all got sick at night from eating too many* (p. 6).

The old Colony Mennonites told Jacob of a job at Aberdeen, Sask. about sixty-five miles from Hague. He went there and got a job with a farmer, Jim Walter, for sixty-five dollars per month. Jim was an Englishman, so Jacob had to get along in English which he did. His boss gave him two dollars extra for stooking.

Jacob finished stooking, then took the train to Hague to see his family at Reinfeldt. He was to go back for threshing in a couple days, but heavy rains came and lasted for several weeks.

Later when it finally cleared, he drove back by buggy. They threshed only one load of wheat, enough to pay him, before it rained again.

In December of 1925 Jacob Friesen agreed to farm together with two other families, the Brauns and the Mantlers. It was a large farm near Saskatoon that had a big house and a small house. The Mantlers lived in the small house and the Braun family lived in the main part of the big house. Elizabeth writes:

> *We lived in part of the big house and another family lived in the main part. They had a boy, Willie, a bit older than I, a very pampered and spoiled boy... the baby of the family. Pants were made with a flap, and I had to button his flap. My brother Jake, who was younger, could do his, but not Willie!*
>
> *One morning I came over early for Willie, and the woman carried him from bed and stood him on a chair in front of the cook stove (it was winter) and completely stripped him and dressed him. I stood amazed! This didn't happen in our home.... We were taught more modesty and to dress ourselves.*
>
> *Willy and we played together a lot. We were the only kids on the farm, the rest were adults. He was very bossy. I remember the barn with lots of cows. We'd go there at milking time sometimes and the milker would squirt milk into the cat's*

mouth and of course at us too. I remember playing in the hayloft too and going along when Dad was hauling hay....

Hedy Mary was born in this house (Feb.17, 1926). That morning Mom scrubbed all the floors. Everything had to be nice and clean. In the evening a lady came, she must have been a nurse, and us kids were taken to the home of the... Mantlers.... I remember how they tucked us into bed, thick feather beds.... In the morning we had a new sister named after the nurse. She was German.

The farm was run on a share basis.... The farming together didn't work. Each of the men knew best and wanted to be boss.

In those days, these immigrants could rent a whole farm, equipment, and everything, just walk in and do the work. Opportunities were handed to them "on a platter" so to speak. Too many of them messed it up and the custom was dropped. It hurt Mom; People should be trustworthy and appreciative (p. 7).

This arrangement didn't last until spring. Maybe there was too much selfishness on the part of some so that working together became impossible. Years later Justina related to her children how the one woman would rush out to the barn earlier than the others and quickly milk the easiest cows leaving the hardest ones for her to milk. This unfair behavior didn't promote a climate of co-operation.

Elizabeth continues with her childhood memories:

Once we lived in a town. One night I awoke from a ruckus and made out that Mom had locked the door and Dad and Uncle John wanted in. They had gone out on the town earlier in the evening. She wouldn't let them in, said they were drunk. They denied it. After some argument she let them in. It must have been alright for I went back to sleep again.

Mostly we lived in the country. One place we had a horse named Star. Star was so tame, we played under her, ran circles around her legs and slid down her rump. She let us do anything. One morning we found her dead in a corner of the pasture

> *across from some neighbors. Their children claimed her, they lived closer, our house was farther away so she was theirs. We had a verbal war. We went home very hurt.*
>
> *These people had several odd-shaped stones near their house. They were oblong shaped like a mound, like they were made of plaster or cement, maybe a couple feet high and a couple feet wide and then longer, smooth, and white. The grass grew around them and trees in the background. We played on them, and those kids told us all sorts of stories about them. Later in time I figured they must have been graves* (p. 7).

For the summer of 1926 Jacob Friesen got a job on Mr. Van Horne's farm near Oyen, Alberta. This farm had two sets of buildings. The Friesen family inhabited the little old house which had a barn nearby and a slough. Elizabeth recorded some vivid memories of this place:

> *That summer we had the measles. Mrs. Van Horne came and sort of took over. She darkened the room, made us stay in bed, and I resented her taking all our clothes off. I hung on to some of them, but we were too sick to resist for long. She came over often to check on us and brought us goodies....*
>
> *One day brother Jake thought he should have a little extra syrup. The pail was sitting on the pantry floor, and he proceeded to dip his finger in and have a lick. Mom caught him unawares and, in his surprise, he jerked and got his hand in up to his elbow and upset the pail. Poor Jake, woe to him! After a scolding, he was sent to the slough to wash. He sat there on his haunches swishing his hand in the water and crying.*
>
> *We had so much fun on that place, exploring... the barn and the yard. We found a snake with oodles of young ones, a whole nest. When we disturbed them the big one swallowed the little ones* (p. 9).

4

Starting Afresh

> *So, Abram moved his tents and went to live near the great trees of Mamre at Hebron, where he built an altar to the Lord.* – Genesis 13:18 NIV.

That fall Jacob Friesen bought his first farm from a bachelor, Mr. Bill McIntosh at New Brigden, north of Oyen. It was a half section (320 acres) with a one room shack, some machinery, eight horses, two cows and one sow. When the family moved in it was already cold and windy. Justina worked hard to get the one room winterized.

Two years after leaving their old home in Ischalka, the wandering family was finally settled in their own home once again, and this time they were landowners! It felt good! The new country was good to them and held a lot of promise!

The little one-roomed shack was crowded. Elizabeth writes:

> *Some of us kids had to sleep on the table in front of the only window. One morning we tussled too much, and Neta fell through. I remember the excitement, the blood and glass. I don't think it left any scars though.*
>
> *Later they moved a one-room house on. It was a good house and nice looking but small. Dad built a kitchen, a small bedroom, and a porch on to it* (p. 10).

Friesen family in 1928, finally in their own home at New Brigden, left to right: Elizabeth, Jacob, Jake, Neta, Justina behind Tena & Hedy in the chair

Justina, remembering the terror and suffering in Russia, never regretted the move, but her husband did get very homesick many times.

By this time Jacob had learned to get along quite well in English. He was quite extroverted and had a knack for learning languages. If he didn't know a word, he would use his hands and body in such a way that he would be understood.

The next summer on June 19, 1927, Tena June was born in their new home at New Brigden. In her Memoirs, she looks back to the conditions that prevailed in the year of her birth:

> *It was a time when the average income was about $1,118.00 a year; a three-bedroom house cost about $4,825.00; a new Ford car cost $495.00; gas cost $.07 a liter; and Canada's population was about 9,637,000. Mackenzie King was Canada's Prime Minister. The old age pension was a first. Transatlantic phone service between U.K. and Canada was also a first. The best movie was "Seventh Heaven", and the favorite tunes were "Ain't She Sweet", "I'm Looking Over a Four-Leafed Clover", and "Ol' Man River"* (Tena, p.18).

The farm offered plenty of opportunity for the growing children to learn to work as they were able. They would go out on the prairie with their mother and a team of horses and wagon to collect." cow chips" or dried dung to be used as fuel for cooking and baking. These cow chips burned quickly, and it took a full load of them to do a week's baking. They built an outdoor oven like the ones they had in Russia.

Starting School

The following year it was time for the children to start school. To reach the school they had to pass through a creek that, during spring thaw, would rise to cover the buggy floorboards. Elizabeth reminisces about early school days:

> *In April 1928, Jake and I started school at McConnell School, a country school two-and one-half miles away. We drove, rode horseback, walked or were taken. Our first day at school, Dad brought us. We didn't know a word of English. The teacher was a man, a Mr. G.P. Freebury.... I was scared. The teacher got the necessary information from Dad and when it came to my name, he wanted to know how to spell it. Dad says, "Oh just write it." At home I was called "Liese." That's the name he gave, so my name came to be spelled "Lisa."*
>
> *When I learned the German and how my name was spelled, I switched to "Liese." I was thirteen years old before I found out my real name was "Elizabeth," was I angry, and humiliated that they had not taught me my right name!*
>
> *That first while in school I cried, and I cried. One day when the teacher had the class up front for oral arithmetic and he asked me a problem, I cried and he said more sternly something like "Come on, you know the answer, stop crying and tell me!" I stopped crying and gave him the right answer. After that it went okay.*
>
> *I remember Arbor Day when we cleaned the school and raked the yard. We had a wiener roast, and then went on a nature hike, the best day of the year. I learned to like Mr. Freebury, and when he left, I cried again. I remember a*

> *Halloween party he gave us at someone's home. It was probably our first. We had fun (p. 8).*

On their first day of school, Art Gillespie, a fellow student, got into a dispute with Jake out in the horse barn, and in anger, chopped a hole in the blanket the children used to cover themselves as they rode to school on that cold April day. Jake complained to the teacher. Art denied that he did it and said Jake did it.

At home Jake told his dad. After supper, his dad took Jake and the blanket to Gillespie's place.

Mr. Gillespie called court to order in his house. Jake made the accusation. Then Art gave his defense. Then Jake gave his rebuttal, after which Art was allowed his rebuttal. Then Mr. Gillespie pronounced Art guilty. He bought Friesens a new blanket, and Art had to use the old one (From a conversation with Jake Friesen, 1992).

Understanding Horses

The children became very much bonded to the horses. Elizabeth writes about them:

> *We liked the horses and spent a lot of time with them. Their names were: Chuck and Kate, Nellie and Baldy, Babe and Mac, Ted and Barney.... We learned to ride on Baldy. Once we could ride, every horse had to be rideable. We learned to ride, work and drive horses.* (p.9)
>
> *The first colt we had was born to Nellie. We named him "Tony." A nice bay and tame, we loved him. One day at school we saw Dad come riding on him. The snow was so deep he couldn't buck.... Then in the spring Dad sold him for forty dollars. We cried and kissed him goodbye.*
>
> *The next round there were three colts. but Kate's died. I cried over that too. It died down in the flat... and when I came for the cows, I would ride to it and cry, poor Kate would come and whinny over her dead colt. It was so sad. The other two were "Prince", born to Babe and "Polly" born to Nellie. Prince was unusual, he was yellow with black feet, mane, tail, and the*

insides of his ears. His face was white. He was like his mother, not very tame. Polly was like her mother, a nice horse.

When I tried chasing the horses home on horseback and Babe was in the group, if she didn't want to go home, she'd kick at me, and I couldn't bring them home. I can't say I liked her very well.

For a while Mom was driving us to and from school. She used Nellie. Mom liked her horses nice and fat. She kept Nellie that way. Mom's father was a lover of good horses and kept the best. Maybe she inherited some of her love of horses from him.

Nellie had a fault, she shied very easily. One day Mom was coming to get us from school. She was late and we had started to walk. We saw her coming and scrunched down in some bushes beside the road. When she got close, we stood up suddenly. Nellie was spooked. She wheeled around with a snort and took off. Mom also was taken by surprise and lost control over her. The buggy was smashed. Luckily, Mom was only bruised. When Nellie stopped, she stood there head high, looking and snorting. Unthinking kids! We were so sorry, but it was too late.

We gathered up the pieces and Mom started riding Nellie home. Some men we knew came along in a car and gave Mom a ride home. We had to walk and lead Nellie home. She shied and snorted at that spot in the road every time she came by for a long time afterwards....

I was riding Nellie looking for the horses one summer day.... I was having trouble locating them. I was riding along at a fair clip when I heard my name called. I slowed down and looked all around. There was a rushing sound with it too, not a soul in sight, open country all around. I thought of an airplane, but no, that's noisy. This was a quiet "whoosh." There was a hawk sailing high in the sky, but she was too far away. I puzzled over it and decided I better just ride slow.

I found the horses, but Babe didn't want to go home. She kicked at me. No matter what angle I tried she always got in the way and kicked, so I couldn't bring them home. Then Dad had to go and bring them. For this reason, we kids wanted to keep Babe at home and ride her to get the horses.

One day I was riding her to bring another unwilling horse in. We came to a corner in the fence; the other horse wheeled around and took off for home. Babe did too on two legs. I lost my balance and slid off, hitting my head on a rock. I think I was knocked out for a bit. I got up slowly, felt groggy and dizzy but walked home. Someone came to meet me. The horses were home already. I just went to the house.... (pp.10, 11).

Harvest Time

In those days, farmers did not yet have mobile grain threshing machines that we know as "combines." They all depended upon large stationary threshing machines to separate the kernels from the straw. First, the farmers cut their ripe grain with a "binder." This was a machine pulled by horses that cut an eight or ten-foot-wide swath of grain and, with the help of a mechanical knotter, tied it into little bundles, hence the name "binder." This machine would be pulled round and round the field cutting a strip each time until it reached the middle.

Then the farmer and his helpers, often his wife and kids or hired hands, would place the bundles in little "stooks" of eight to twelve bundles leaning upright against each other. These stooks were usually placed in neat long rows. A good crop, well stooked, looked quite pleasing to the eye and suggested a well-organized farmer.

The threshing machine, or grain separator, resembled a dinosaur for size and shape. From feeder to blower, it was about thirty feet long and stood on four large wheels. Its body reached about ten feet from the ground. The side profile of the feeder resembled a beak, with its hooded mouth raised like a head, which was filled with iron teeth that moved up and down in a gigantic chewing motion.

It had a big bulky body that was filled with rotating cylinders, shakers, sieves, and air-gulping fans on the inside, and had a network of pullies and belts on the outside to power them. At the backside, it had a rounded rump topped by an awkward blower that stuck up and out at one corner, like a lopsided tail.

A threshing machine was very expensive, so most farmers did not own one. A big farmer might buy one, and then would do threshing for hire, which would help him pay for the machine.

It was common for such a machine to be busy from mid-August until late November, when winter set in, or even in spring, if winter arrived before they were finished. The farmer would also have a steam engine or a very big tractor to pull the threshing machine from farm to farm, and to power it during threshing.

A farmer, who was to have his grain threshed, arranged with twelve to sixteen of his neighbors to help him, in turn for his help when their turn to thresh came.

When threshing day came, the machine would be brought in and positioned beside a granary or at a selected spot with a grain-wagon in place. The tractor that brought it would be turned around to face the machine at an appropriate distance. It was lined up and connected to the thresher with a very long and heavy drive belt. The tractor then served as a stationary engine with pully in motion, driving the threshing machine.

Threshing at each farm might take several days. The farmer, where the crew was working, was expected to feed them all.

The neighbors would gather, each with a team of horses and an open wagon. They would go out to the field where people known as "field pitchers," with three-pronged pitchforks, would load the bundles onto the wagon until it was full.

The teams would bring the loaded wagons to the front of the threshing machine alongside the feeder. As they pitched the bundles into the feeder, the feeder chain would slowly move them into the mouth of the giant "dinosaur" where mechanical teeth chewed up the bundles which were then swallowed into its rumbling, shaking belly.

Puffs of smoke-like dust would blow out of every crack or bolt hole in the body of this rumbling monster. Out of a spout, somewhere near the center of this machine, a steady stream of golden grain would pour into the granary or into a grain-wagon box.

At the tail end of this monster was a blower pipe about twenty-five feet long and eighteen inches in diameter sticking out from the top, at about a forty-five-degree angle, into the air. Out of this pipe blew a steady stream of the waste products of this monster's endless meal, dust and golden straw, which piled up in a huge mound until it often reached twenty-five to thirty feet high.

Great caution needed to be exercised. Even if a small spark would touch this straw stack, it could ignite, and in a matter of minutes, burn the straw, the grain, the machinery, and sometimes, even the stubble in the field. The old steam engines had a habit of discharging sparks from their smokestacks or their fire boxes. Many a harvest was lost through carelessness. Sometimes enemies settled scores by torching the other's stack at night. Thoughtless children sometimes played with matches or experimented with fire or played a "prank" which resulted in the sudden loss of a straw stack.

The women of the home were equally involved. A few of the neighbor women would come to help. Feeding twelve to sixteen hard-working hungry men three meals on the same day, plus providing morning and afternoon snacks to these men in the field, was no small task.

Tena wrote an insider's view:

> *As soon as we heard which day it was to be our turn, Mom and my older sisters went into action. They got ready.... All three meals were generally served at the same time of day at each place. Time saved was money earned. The dinners were the busiest. Large amounts of mashed potatoes formed in an artsy mountain-shaped form topped with melted butter, a large gravy bowl full of home-made gravy, large thick slices of baked home-cured ham, fresh creamed vegetables and onions from the garden, jam, jelly, and home-made butter, home-made bread and buns fresh from the oven, and Mom's home-made apple pie topped with a generous portion of cheddar cheese were all placed on a well-set table in large amounts.*
>
> *We listened and watched from the kitchen window, and we could tell when it was quitting time. Sharp on the hour the machines shut down, and in a short time, the hungry dusty men walked in briskly from the field. Some were bent a little, some were bow-legged, but all were pleasant ordinary men. They washed up in a tin basin on a table outside with great gusto. They slicked down their hair with a large comb....*

> *The food was on the table. We were ready to serve. To hear the crew rave about the good food was music to my mother's ears. She deserved every single compliment and more. She always looked so chic in her well-groomed hair, her neatly pressed cotton dress and white apron with a large bow at the back. These men worked with incredible speed, and they ate the same way.... When the men took second helpings it was a sure sign that they liked our food. A certain shy look from a nervous single man was a sure sign that this farmer's daughter really pleased him. Appreciation was a nice reward for lots of hard work with limited amenities....*
>
> *Not only did the crew get three full meals a day, but we also brought their morning and afternoon lunches out to the crew in the field. Sometimes I was allowed to go and at the same time I got to see the live performance of the threshers in action* (pp.130-134).

Those were good years on the prairie and the crops were rewarding. Elizabeth tells about harvesting from a little girl's point of view:

> *At threshing time our neighbor, Mrs. Anderson, helped Mom with the cooking. They were exciting times. Our neighbor, Alf Jorgenson, had the threshing machine. He had a huge tractor and did the threshing in that area. There were at least twelve men on the outfit. Farmers helped each other. They pulled in with a bunk house where they slept and the farmer where they were working fed them. It was an early to late job. They worked hard and ate good. It took much cooking.*
>
> *We loved to play in the new straw stacks. One time we wanted to go up on a new stack they were still threshing on, but Dad said "no." We sneaked around and did anyway. I suppose we had the idea that if we got right under the straw spout it would be real fun. Well, we climbed up; it was a high stack already. We fell right to the bottom, buried in straw. We screamed and kicked. Jake was more levelheaded than Neta or me, and got us quieted down, and we started digging. First,*

he emerged, then me, and we both pulled Neta out. We were thoroughly chastened and walked home very subdued. I don't think our parents ever knew how close they came to losing their kids. We never did it again and were always cautious about new stacks after that (p.12).

Guardian Angels

For an eight-to-ten-year-old girl, Elizabeth was very sensitive, sensible, responsible, and spiritually perceptive. On several occasions she heard voices calling her name which she attributes to the care of "guardian angels." She recalls:

Some summers Dad built an outdoor oven and Mom baked her bread in it. This one time I was bringing stuff to help make the oven. I was running past the house on the west side (front) through the grass and heard my name called. I stopped and listened, but there was no one. I pondered this as I walked the rest of the way to Mom and asked her if she had called me. She said "no." I said, "I heard my name called," and she said, "Maybe it was an angel." I pondered that for a while.

Another time it was a rainy day and us kids were playing in the barn, Mom and Dad were in the house. I ran to the house for something. It was raining and I was running back to the barn. Coming around the corner of the house I heard my name called. I slowed down, listened, and looked all around but there was no one. I started to run again when the voice said with great urgency, "Liese stand still!" I stopped right in the gateway and a bullet whizzed by just at eye level.

I stood there a bit overwhelmed, my eyes following the direction of the bullet. I walked to the barn in deep thought and told my sister and brother. I also told my parents. Dad must have told the neighbors. He came home one day and said the neighbor boys had been shooting coyotes. We had heard shots that day. (p.12).

Fun Times

Despite being restricted by the limitations of poverty, this pioneer family had a lot of fun times during those years. Elizabeth recalls:

> *Another favorite play place was beside the house well. It was a low spot with a stone pile in it and overgrown with buckbrush and other plants. It was usually the greenest spot on the farmstead, and we played there, built our farms, using the buckbrush for trees (p.15).*
>
> *I remember another Halloween, the weather was so nice, with a big moon shining. We had some oat bundle stacks by the barn and we played in there till way late. Our threshing was just finished, and the outfit was moved to the neighbors. Later we heard the thresher men were lurking in the shadows waiting on us kids to go to bed so they could play some pranks, but we stayed up too late. They didn't get much done. Our dog barked and Dad went out to see. He didn't see anything but heard an awful puffing sound like someone was running and dragging something. Next morning, we saw our harrow cart way out in the field. They later confessed our place was too well watched. They didn't do what they wanted to. The neighbors got more mischief done to them* (p.14).

Building an Altar

Worship and church life was very important to the family. There were other Mennonite settlers in the vicinity, so although there was not yet a church building, they agreed to meet in the home of David Wiens, a Sunday school teacher who had been trained as a teacher back in Russia. Elizabeth found their worship gatherings to be very meaningful:

> *We had church maybe once a month in the David Wiens home. It was an all-day affair. Church in the morning and Sunday school in the afternoon with Bible study for the adults and youth, and sometimes choir practice for the youth too. They were good days. I remember the programs especially at*

> *Christmas. In the summers we might have a church picnic with recitations, singing and games. Dad was baptized into the Mennonite Brethren Church on June 14, 1931, at Sedalia. We gathered at a lake for the service and he and some others were immersed* (p. 14).
>
> *Those Christmases! How excited we'd get! Christmas eve was always the Sunday school program. We'd bundle up good and drive to Wiens's where the gathering was. Then with other excited youngsters, we'd give our pieces, sing our songs, and then came the bags and gifts, usually story books. Happy and sleepy, we'd drive home. It was four miles. Not too sleepy to set out our plates for the "Christmas Man." Then to bed and wait for morning. In the cold morning, before the parents were up, we'd go see what we had in our plates and take it to bed with us* (Elizabeth Hansen, unpublished eulogy, "I Remember Mom" (p. 2).

Learning to Work

Children could prove very loyal and useful beyond their years. Children's rights and child labor laws were unknown in those parts. Elizabeth describes some of the errands she was required to perform by the time she was eleven years of age.

> *Sometimes us kids were sent to town on errands. New Brigden was about five miles away and we'd either ride horseback or go in the buggy. One day Dad sent me to mail a letter. The stamp was two cents but when I got there the postmistress, Mrs. Shepherd, said the postage had gone up to three cents. I was sort of nonplussed, but staunchly declared Dad said it was two cents and stuck by that. Anyway, I'm sure I didn't have another penny. Well alright, she said and took the letter. I don't know what she thought of me* (p.14).
>
> *The year 1931 was dry. Our crop was puny. Dad got a job at Cereal building road. He had to use his own horses. All we had at home was Nellie and Baldy, two yearlings and Nellie's suckling colt. One day he sent word to Mom that Jake, and I*

were to hitch up to the wagon and come to Cereal on a certain Saturday. He would be finished his work then and wanted to bring two loads of coal home.

It was twenty miles to Cereal, and we had never been there before. We knew the road as far as the Sedalia turnoff. He left detailed instructions as to how to get there and where to go.

Early Saturday, we started to get ready. We had to patch some harness together as Dad had all the good ones.... We had to go slow because of the colt. We got there late afternoon. We asked some kids where Mr. Friesen was and with some further talk, they pointed to the road gang working out of town. We went there.... When they quit, Dad was bragging us up all over the place. We got the coal loaded and started for home, after the horses had a bit to eat and drink. Dad drove ahead with his team, and we followed.

How long the night was! How many times we fell asleep! How many times we dropped the lines! Good thing that horses go home by themselves. It was about three a.m. when we got home. The longest night in my memory up to that time. Mom welcomed us home. We could only drag off to bed. No church that Sunday! (p.15).

A Shelter in the Time of Storm

A common occurrence on the prairies was storms, thunderstorms, hailstorms, dust storms, snowstorms, and blizzards. Sometimes these make deep impressions on the mind of a child. Elizabeth describes some of them:

One day we were driving home with horses and open wagon. The hail started just before we got home. We hurried up and got in the house just before the heavy stuff came. Mom would hold pillows against the window glass to help keep them from breaking.

Once we and Mom were home alone, it was toward evening when a bad storm came up. It was so bad we were afraid the house would blow away. We felt it tremble. Mom knelt with us and prayed; we were safe.

Another time we kids were home alone. Our parents had gone to some church meeting in the evening. A storm came up. We could feel the house tremble. Mom said later she had gone outside at Wiens's, where the meeting was, and seen how tumultuous the heavens were. She must have prayed for our safety; she didn't say but said she thought of us. The house and we were safe, but the roof blew off the chicken house and most of the chickens were drowned. It rained with the wind. We later found drowned chickens scattered all over, even in the grain field. The wind had sucked them out. We found the roof there too. Mom had raised a hundred chickens from brood hens that spring and she was so happy for them and now one storm took them away.... That was the best chicken crop she ever had. The barn was smashed.

We kids were happy we had turned the horses out. Dad must have been in a big hurry or maybe they were still feeding when they left. Anyway, we went to the barn after our parents left and were surprised to see the horses still in, so we turned them out. There had been a hen setting in one of the mangers in the barn. The morning after the storm we wondered what happened to her, so we went looking and found her still sitting on her eggs safe and sound, the only dry hen on the place. When the wind blew the barn over, the boards fell in such a way as to protect her. There was other destruction too, but the barn and the chickens were the biggest loss. I don't know what it did to the crop. The binder was rolled to the middle of the driveway.

The barn got rebuilt. I remember neighbors helping. Dad had a new well drilled by the new barn. It was sixty feet deep when they hit water. It was done with a rig where the horses went round and round. I remember the backslapping when they hit water. The water wasn't as good as the house well which was close to the road north of the house. It was good water but not enough for livestock and human consumption as well (p. 15).

Our stove pipe was real long, right across the kitchen. One windy day I remember the pipe getting red hot and how worried

> *Mom was and how she worked to get the fire down. She used wet clothes to cool the pipe down* (p. 14).
>
> *We must have had great dust storms that I don't remember but the sand built up along the fence lines along the road nearly to the top of the fence posts. We kids would play in this sand* (p. 15).

Tena was impressed with the sandstorms and drought conditions as a five or six-year-old child. Looking back, she vividly describes those times:

> *Year after year the slow, steady, hot, searing, sucking winds came, and... blew away the sandy topsoil. Even as I watched I could see the earth disappear. The rains never came. This had never happened here before, but it could happen again. Even if the crops looked promising at first, the hot winds soon reduced them to nothing. Our crops and gardens just went with the wind.*
>
> *Sometimes the early crops froze, or later a cloud of grasshoppers reduced them to nothing. Even the stubble didn't survive this invasion. The only thing that could control grasshoppers was a cold wet spring and we never had one....*
>
> *My mother tried to keep the dust out of our house by covering the windows, but the fine dust still crept into our home in large amounts. The washing went out white and came in grey. The winds dried our lips and nostrils, and turned our eyes red. The only remedies we had were ointment and vaseline.*
>
> *During the "dirty thirties" the skies became hazy and heavily laden with dust. The searing winds put a pink dusty haze into the earth's atmosphere which was visible all over the world. Planes flew around or over it. Only the tumble weed survived and for no good purpose. I watched it roll out of sight or until something stopped it like a fence. A viable way of life died in front of our eyes, and we couldn't do anything about it.... It was the same kind of suffering for everybody. It formed a common bond that held people together....* (Tena Friesen, pp. 39-44).

Sturdy Stuff

During those years two more baby girls were added to the family; Helen Betty, born on February 10, 1929, and Melita Jessie, born on April 9, 1930. These two were born in the hospital at Cereal, Alberta.

It is almost unbelievable nowadays how pioneer women had to work in those tough times. Justina worked as hard as the best. Through those years they moved at least fifteen times or on an average of once every eighteen months. Each time they moved she would have to clean up a dirty abandoned house, fix it up, and make it into a home for her growing family.

She would always make big and wonderful gardens, tend them, and harvest them and preserve the produce. Besides that, she was expected to help with field work when needed. Of course, she taught her growing children by delegating and supervising them in sharing the responsibilities of the work.

There was the daily chores of milking cows, feeding pigs and chickens, collecting eggs, etc., not to mention cooking three meals a day, baking bread for her large family every day, cleaning house, making clothes, washing clothes by hand, hanging them out to dry, bringing them in when dry, mending clothes, ironing clothes with the old "sad irons" that had to be heated and reheated on the hot stove before wash-and-wear was ever heard of, darning socks, knitting sweaters, carrying clean water in and garbage water out, collecting cow chips or chopping wood for fuel, tending the fire when cooking or baking or when it was cold, churning butter, and selling butter and eggs. They all worked together, but it was Justina who coordinated and took responsibility to see that all was done and done right.

Besides all this, she must take time to be a real mother to each of her children, feed them, bath them, dress them, listen to them, teach them, tell them stories, tend to their hurts, comfort them, care for them when they were sick, solve their problems, answer their questions, and give them the guidance they needed.

And while doing all these duties, she managed to produce another new healthy baby every nineteen months on the average. In remembering, her children praised her:

> *I remember the threshing times, the meals. She usually fed them her own grown chicken, goose, or turkey. The threshers looked*

forward to coming, for here they got a change in meat. One time especially, the threshers came sooner than expected and we weren't ready. She didn't know what to give for dessert. She sent me to the neighbor lady for something. The lady said, "Why don't you give them pumpkin pie?" And she gave me a recipe. We didn't know a thing about pumpkin pie, but we made it. Mom griped the whole time; sure, this couldn't be anything. The threshers relished the huge slabs of pie and didn't leave any for her or me. They really complimented her on it.

Who won't remember Mom's baking! Almost every day she baked huge loaves of bread. Years later, when I'd come home, I could just eat and eat her cooking. The way she made gravy from almost nothing and poured it over potatoes cooked in their jackets, was a treat.

People complimented her on how white she washed her old wooden floors. After I started to work out, I said, "No wonder they can't get their floors white, they just use mops." We scrubbed on hands and knees.

Mom always had flowers. If there was a garden, there were flowers in it. "Something for the soul", she'd say. "Man shall not live by bread alone," and she didn't.

I remember how she'd tell us stories. We only had church once a month, and the other Sundays, especially, she'd tell us stories. How quiet and peaceful those Sundays seemed to be. She gave us a good knowledge of the Bible, taught us Bible verses, memory work for Sunday school, songs, and poems for special occasions like Christmas, etc. We were often complimented for our reciting ability. She also taught us German. Perish the thought that we should not learn our mother tongue!

One of her mottoes might have been: "I have to live for my children!" When she'd go for a little rest sometimes, she could mentally shut the noise off and rest. Amid all the noise and racket, she would sit down with her Bible and have her little quiet time. I remember this especially on winter evenings. Sometimes I watched her covertly. Once in particular, she was sitting at the end of our rough table, the coal oil lamp in front of her, shading her eyes from the lamp with her hand, she read her Bible. I saw the tears fall which she carefully wiped away. We were not to see. Here she met her God, here she "refueled", her trysting place. "Lord, I have shut the door, strengthen my heart; yonder awaits the task, I share a part. Only by grace bestowed may I be true; Here while alone with Thee, my strength renews!"

In all the hardships and disappointments Mom suffered, she always forgave and tried again. Always somehow, she scratched up new hope. A proverb she often quoted: "Wen hofnung nicht wer dan lebt man nicht mer." ["If hope wasn't, we wouldn't live anymore!] (Elizabeth Hansen, unpublished eulogy, "I Remember Mom")

Tena adds in the same vein:

When my father saw he was losing everything that he ever worked for he became a disillusioned and angry man. It was my mother who showed tremendous inner strength, great courage, and great faith in her God to see us through. She was extremely stoic, and her role model overwhelmed me. Words come easy to people, but to say, "We'll start over!" over, and over again, and mean it, is something else! Many people's loss during the Great Depression was so great and devastating it destroyed the spirit. Many had come here from Europe, seeking a better land only to lose it to the dust after finding it. It was the same for many in those days (pp. 45-46).

Destiny afforded my mother only a poor simple harsh life. She never complained. Her life was having babies, kneading dough, baking bread, washing clothes by hand, scrubbing floors on her knees, and canning the garden stuff after she brought it all to fruition. Her life was flour sacks and homemade lye soap. What was written on my parents faces was put there by emotions and heritage. It was an era when unbelievable things were happening every day (p. 58).

Helen remembers her mother's German Bible Story Book with pictures in it, and how she would look at the pictures and ask her mother about the pictures and that would bring a story. She also remembers how she loved the soups her mother made. There was "*ludic*" made from a wild plant, and milk soups, and "R*evil*" soup served with toast. She recalls:

> *Jake wasn't that fond of soup. At least not the one kind Mom made. I recall Dad telling him if you eat that I'll give you a dollar. I think Jake ate the soup but never saw the dollar.*

5

Surviving Drought

Now there was a famine in the land, and Abram went down to Egypt to live there for a while because the famine was severe. – Genesis 12:10

The year was 1931, and the good years were over. The stock market crashed in 1929; the "Great Depression" was tightening its stranglehold on the economic world; a great drought was turning the western plains into a giant "dust bowl," and the decade into the "dirty thirties." Elizabeth recalls the effect these tough times had on their lives:

> *Dad was a person afflicted with the wanderlust. It seems he could never stay in one spot for long. The dry years had started, and Dad looked for greener pastures. At harvest time, he was off somewhere. Mom and Jake looked after the harvest. We threshed 200 bushels of grain that year.... When Dad came home, he'd found a place at Chinook. The crops there were a little better that year.*
>
> *Dad sold our farm, and one evening in November we loaded all our stuff on our neighbor Anderson's farm truck, and we moved to Chinook. We moved into a new little three-roomed house with a closed in porch. We were so crowded. It was a very cold, cold place with very thin walls in a cold winter.*
>
> *Anita Helen was born in this house on January 8, 1932.... Two neighbor women came to help, and we were chucked off to one of them and babysat their child. It was blustery cold, wind and snow. It was a long day.*

Dad found a farm two miles north of Chinook we could have. It had a huge house on it, but all the inside walls were torn out. The story was that a brother and two sisters had lived on it.... The brother had died, and the sisters lost the farm. It now belonged to a company. The sisters waged a legal battle but lost and had to leave. Out of vengeance they proceeded to destroy the place. They tore out the walls, ceilings, even floors upstairs. One room downstairs got missed. They lived in that room and used the wood from the rest for fuel. They destroyed tree plantings and garden shrubs.... It used to be a real show place.... because of the destruction, the company had a hard time renting it.... So far as I know the company provided the materials to put in walls.

Dad spent the winter putting in walls and floors etc. I don't remember when we moved in, probably in spring as Mother put in a garden. I remember helping. It sure was nice, lots of room, a beautiful location, a large grass area around the house and garden, great for a bunch of children. I remember learning to help mother and babysitting for the neighbors. I remember the Johnsons north of us. I babysat their children on several occasions. I liked to go there. Their oldest child, Marjorie and I would make the beds, tidy the house, whatever Mrs. would let us do, and we had so much fun doing it (pp.15,16).

The two sisters that used to live there were living in Chinook and a neighbor girl knew them. So, one noon hour we went to visit them. They were getting up in years and were rather old-fashioned, wearing their hair combed up and into a bun on the top of their heads. We had a nice visit and they invited us back, but I don't think we ever went back again. As it goes with these kinds of people, all sorts of weird stories circulated about them (p. 17).

School Days

Moving meant adjusting to a new school situation also. Elizabeth remembers:

My best school experience was in Chinook. Jake and I were in grade three when we moved there. Since we started in spring we didn't get promoted with the other kids. When the inspector came, he was the same man they had at McConnell. He recognized us and promoted me to grade four in May.... If I learned the long division, multiplication, subtraction and adding, I could go to grade five in September. I did it. I had a good teacher who spent extra time with me. She seemed so pleased to do it.... She was Isabel Matheson, the best schoolteacher I have ever had.

We had a test. Anyone who scored over eighty got their paper back. I was sitting at the end of the row and one day the teacher came walking down the aisle with a paper. Naturally, I thought it was for the boy in front of me, but she handed it to me and shamed the boy for being in the class the whole year and me only a short while. I felt sorry for him, still do, who knows what his life outside of school was. That fall I was in grade five. I don't know why they didn't move Jake up too. I thought he was smarter than I. Possibly he had to miss too much school to help Dad.

At Chinook we drove to school in horse drawn vans. I remember how cold we'd get in winter. We had some awfully poky drivers, they just let the horses walk all the way and it took so long to get home. The farmers took turns driving. They worked their school taxes off this way, I think.

Our turn to drive school van came in June,1933. I had to do it. It was a dry year and Dad had gone off to look for greener pastures. He left us with enough feed for these two horses and we were to keep them in and drive the van. We had a very sober school principal. Imagine my apprehension when he came to the van after school one day and asked if that was the way it was supposed to be, pointing to the harness. A strap was loose, and Jake got out quickly and fastened it.

The principal came to see if I'd be driving next day and give me some directions concerning van service it being sports day next day. Not so bad after all. I rather think I was driving illegally, being too young.

There were only four kids beside us on this van and two boys were older than I, high school age if I remember right. It was exam time in June, and they didn't always come. They were very respectful, so I had no behavior problem (pp. 17, 18).

Dad got me a red hat and the boys teased me with being a "red-headed woodpecker", sometimes changed it to "red-wooded head pecker!" (pp. 16, 17).

Farm Work

Farm work became more demanding for the growing children. Elizabeth recalls:

Jake and I worked very hard here at Chinook. Before harvest Dad had acquired another section of land with the crop on. It was 1932. Jake and I stooked all the crop that year, must have been about 800 acres. I don't know how heavy the crop was, but I know we worked hard. It was so hot and dry day after day and what nosebleeds we had!

In this deal, Dad got a section of land two miles west of the town of Chinook, fourteen horses, two cows, and some pigs. The railroad and Highway No. 9 ran through this farm. It was called the DeMann farm. After harvest he let the company farm go. We moved before harvest. The house had five rooms. This is where Annie Irma was born on April 30, 1933 (p. 17).

We had fourteen horses with this farm, and in our mind each one had to be ridden. If they were not used to it, we made sure they got used to it. The summer of 1933 was so dry pastures dried up, even wells. Before Dad left, he told us to pasture the horses on the grain fields across the tracks. He went to Duchess to work and to look for a place to live. Twice every day we had to bring the horses in to water at the buildings.... The gates across the tracks had to be kept closed.

Every horse had to have his turn.... There was one we called "Jack" who didn't ride. Nothing daunted Jake and Henry Neufeld... who spent a whole day getting him used to it. By evening we could ride Jack too.

In two years at Chinook, we lived on three different farms. In 1933 we dried out completely; no crop, no garden, no money,

> *no nothing, and nothing to do. For once Mother could enjoy (?) leisure. She said that of all her babies she played with Annie the most* (p. 18).

Even the small children had to do their share of the work. Helen explains:

> *There was a long narrow lean-to against the barn where the wood and cow chips (dry cow dung) were stored. Across the road was a lease where cattle and horses roamed. We girls went there with pails and a little wagon and filled them with chips and stored them in this shed. So that provided us with fuel.*

One day a visitor was bragging about how good he was at barbering. Justina allowed him to demonstrate his skills on Helen. He made such a mess of it that, after he left, her mother shaved her head. Little four-year-old Helen was so embarrassed that she wore a red toque which she refused to take off.

Sometime later a visiting lady coaxed her to show her how it looked under the toque. With some encouragement from her mother, Helen finally relented and took it off. Then the women both admired how nice her hair looked, so she decided to leave the toque off.

A Church at Chinook

There were Mennonites in this community as well. There was a Funk family just across the road from the company farm. They had seven children. A church was started, as Elizabeth describes:

> *On the DeMann farm was a second house, a small one which the church people converted into our church house. It was convenient for us, but we also had to do the janitor work. At Chinook we had a minister and so regular services. Up to then the services had been in the homes of the families by turns.*
>
> *We had worship services in the morning and Sunday school in the afternoon while the adults had Bible study. It was an all-day affair; people brought their dinners along.... The two oldest Funk boys were especially good on the violin. They*

> *usually performed at school concerts and at church programs. I greatly enjoyed these activities. We often recited, especially for Christmas.*
>
> *We had a good minister. He paid special attention to the children, especially to the young boys. He'd call them to the front bench in church and, throughout his sermon, ask them a question occasionally, thus keeping their attention* (p. 17).
>
> *My worst frustration came from Fritz. He was a grade ahead of me in the same age bracket. Seems we were always in competition. We went to the same Sunday school. If I knew two verses, he'd come with three the next Sunday. He was smart and always had to have the right answers* (p. 18).

Then Fritz's father, Mr. Peters, died. He was a neighbor just north of the Friesen's. According to their custom, Justina made a pair of slippers for his burial using a shoe box for the soles. Helen remembers his funeral:

> *He was laid out in a granary. He was not in the church, and he did not lay in a coffin like we use now. It was like the pictures from Russia. I thought this man was sleeping, but I couldn't figure out why all the ladies were so busy arranging flowers, etc. However, the body was taken into the Church for the funeral service.*

The Drought

By this time, the drought had intensified its strangle hold on the dryland prairie farmers. They watched their once green farms turn into one vast "dust bowl", and their hopes blow away with their soil. Those whose roots were less deep were abandoning their farms and trekking off to greener places. Tena vividly describes her childhood memories of those times:

> *By 1932 the steady hot winds wrapped everything in a huge cloud of dust. Millions of acres in North America were destroyed, and the topsoil was nearly all blown away from millions of more acres. Even though the warning signs of soil erosion were there for years the farmers didn't have the finances to prevent it. They worked the land to the limit regardless of*

> *the dangers of depleting their natural resources and abilities to recover. Governments and farmers had not yet heard of contour plowing. This method came much too late for my folks and many other farmers.*
>
> *This was dryland. Year after year the drought continued. There was no rain. Every day my father and brother Jake measured and watched the well water levels drop. They gazed up to search for some sign, but all they saw was a hot hazy sun promising more of the same. I don't remember if winters didn't bring enough snow, but I do know the sun shone hot year after year just burning up the land around us, and that we were getting poorer and poorer. By the mid-thirties dusty hazy skies could be seen all over the world. A whole way of life died before our very own eyes....*
>
> *Farming became a slow way of starving. Even the toughest of farmers bowed to the elements and quit.... I remember a dust storm lasting for four days, and there was legitimate concern for our own safety if the storm lasted too long.*
>
> *We kept the lantern lit all day as the dust darkened the day. I was afraid of being buried alive in deep sand. When this storm abated, I picked one of our large red hens out of a sand drift. Our hens, birds, and some animals died in this storm. They smothered to death in thick drifts of sand. The drifts filled coulees and valleys, and buried fences. Large rolls of dry prickly Russian thistle blew across the land leaving prickly thistle half buried in deep sand along the way* (Tena Friesen, pp. 39-44).

While the hopes of the prairie farmers were dashed by the drought and buried in the dust, the rest of the world fared little better in the grip of "The Great Depression." After the stock market "crashed" in 1929, the prices of farm produce vanished. Where grain or produce grew, it didn't pay the costs of harvesting. Many crops were left in the fields to rot while millions elsewhere did not have enough to eat. There was no money to pay the costs of the transportation.

Many farmers could not pay their mortgages and abandoned their farms. They went to the cities in search of a better life, but there was no work. Many became homeless, wandering from place to place on foot or by bumming rides on freight trains. They would come around offering to work for food.

Children were often malnourished. Many of them never knew what an apple or an orange tasted like. Tena says: "We could never afford to buy fruit, but our local storekeeper gave us some oranges for Christmas every year in return for our patronage" (p. 39).

She admires how her parents coped:

> *My parents were proud people. They came from very strong stock. We are survivors. Those times were very difficult. We survived on sourdough bread baked in a pan, over potatoes as dumplings, or fried until the spring brought fresh greens to our table. My mother had her ways of serving a tasty meal. She used onions, wild herbs, and spices for flavor. She had many ways of preparing potatoes, eggs, sourdough, and soups. It was never easy for many people, but they shared everything they had with their neighbors without malice or in trepidation* (pp. 40-41).

6

Surviving the Great Depression

> *I was standing on the bank of the Nile, when out of the river there came up seven cows, fat and sleek, and they grazed among the reeds. After them, seven other cows came up – scrawny and very ugly and lean. I had never seen such ugly cows in all the land of Egypt. The lean, ugly cows ate up the seven fat cows that came up first. But even after they ate them, no one could tell that they had done so; they looked just as ugly as before.* – Genesis 41:17-24 NIV.

Mennonites from Chinook and New Brigden were moving north to places like Tofield and the Peace River country where there was more rainfall. Jacob Friesen went southwest to investigate the opportunities for finding a better life in the Rosemary or Duchess community in the Eastern Irrigation District.

Neta Broadfoot shares her memory of the move that followed:

> *The year was 1933. The season was the end of August. There were eleven of us altogether on our farm three miles west of Chinook, Alberta: Dad and Mother and nine children between the ages of thirteen years to four months. This was the third farm we had lived on within two years.*

The summer was so hot and dry with scorching winds. The ground and sandy places so hot we nearly burnt our bare feet when walking about. We'd hunt shady spots to play in.

The garden had a few dried-up plants, while the crops grew to about eight inches high and dried up, thin yellow stems with empty little heads. We children tried to get kernels of wheat, but there were none. It was always fun to chew on wheat, making "chewing gum," which was the only kind of gum we could afford. None this year!

Grasshoppers in clouds came to devour what little was left. You could hear them munching away on the vegetation. Poison was put out to kill them but to no avail. Dad, coming home from scouting around for a new place, informed us, "We're going to move again!"

We were all excited to think of moving to another farm over one hundred miles away. What a great distance that seemed to us children! Mother must have been so tired of moving, knowing how much work was involved. Dad and Mother, with the help of the older children, of which I was one, loaded up the hayrack with all our possessions.

Dad made a crate to go across the center of the rack for our thirty chickens. There was a little booth made in the center of the front half of the rack for mother and the little ones to sit out of the sun and wind. At the back we loaded the small stove to cook on, the cream separator, bedsteads, and our one little pig in a crate. Our cow came behind, tied to the back of the rack with her calf following.

Before we left, we all toured the house for the last time, bidding good-bye to all that had transpired there. The good times and the not-so-good ones.

At last, we were moving. It was about Aug. 25th. On the way, I remembered I had left my tin tea box with all my Sunday school cards and verses on a shelf in the bedroom, all my earthly treasures. How I begged mother to run back and get them, but mother would not hear of it. She consoled me with "Maybe the next family that lives there will have very little, and their child will love the pictures." What happened to them we will never know.

Jake and Elizabeth each rode a horse alongside, while the heavy work horses pulled the load. It was fun for me and the other children, but real hardship for mother and the little ones, especially four-month-old Annie.

About a half mile down the road going through a steep gully near our neighbors, the back axle broke, due to such a big heavy load. Now what could we do? There was a threshing crew in the field nearby, trying to salvage some grain and straw. They stopped and came and helped Dad fix the axle. I still wanted to go back for my box. I was so sure that I could run back and make it before the axle was fixed, but Mother still would not let me.

That night we stayed at a farm about twelve miles down the road. We were all tired and hungry by now. These kind people gave us supper and we slept on their living room floor on improvised beds. Here we had our first encounter with bed bugs. Ugh!

Next morning, we were on our way again. We traveled across country roads, taking the shortest route. It was hot, the sun beating down on us, the horses needed resting periods. I remember running behind the wagon in the dust, enjoying the trip.

The second night we stayed at an old couple's farm. They also were dried out and had very little. Jake and Elizabeth slept in a granary and the old man locked the door for the night so they couldn't run away. Hedy, Tena, Helen, Melita, and I slept on a rough bed of comforters and blankets on top of the chickens on the rack. What a night! The chickens squawked when any of us moved around, and near morning it started to drizzle, so we got soaked and cold. The bedding was hung on the rack to dry the next day.

Being so many of us, it took a lot of bread. Mother mixed bread and let it rise while traveling and baked it in the stove when we stopped for a rest. No bread ever tasted better.

At one stop there was a water hole where the horses and cow were watered. The calf fell in and was nearly submerged. Dad had Jake go in and put a rope around it to pull it out. Jake started to sink too and went in quite deep. Mother came running, wringing her hands, "Don't let Jake drown, the calf is not worth it!" The calf was pulled out. Jake was none the worse for the wetting, and we could move on again.

We traveled at a good pace, changing the tired team for a fresher one when needed. We had six horses with us, and they were very good horses.

When we reached the banks of the Red Deer River, we met a rancher on a wagon. He stopped and took mother and all the younger one, including myself, on the wagon across the river bridge. This was safer than staying on the rack. The riverbank was steep, but we made it without any mishap.

On we went to our new home, only fourteen miles to go. Our new farm was close by the #1 highway, which we reached just as the evening Greyhound Bus went by. What a sight, our first big bus! We were to become very familiar with seeing the bus go by morning and evening.

We arrived the 1st of September, late in the afternoon at our new home, a four-room CPR house on irrigated land. Tired, damp, and hungry, we quickly unloaded the necessary things, cooked supper, and went to bed. Thus began a new phase of our lives.

Tena also shared a six-year old's memory of that trip in her Memoirs. To her young mind, this was an adventure, not unlike what a modern child would feel enjoying her first cross-country vacation trip in the family's camper. Besides describing in somewhat exaggerated detail the arrangement of the "camper" wagon, she shared her feelings:

Everything we had for our trek across the prairie was on that hayrack. The thought that we were poor and had very little never crossed my mind. This trip was pure adventure and excitement for me. I was six years old, and I didn't know there

> *was anything else involved in our moving away. I had a feeling that finding dead hens in sand was a tragedy, I really did not understand it.*
>
> *It was late August when we started this long trek across the vast stark dry prairie to get to our new place. I had not yet started school and this trek was a major trip for me. I was awed by the vastness of the prairie and the grandeur of the wide-open skies at night, the Milky Way, the fall moon, the dancing Northern lights, the shooting stars, and bursting fireballs are all wonderful sights that I have seen and will always remember. And I shall always remember the hoots of the owls at night, and the eerie howls of the coyotes in the distance.*
>
> *Each day twice a day... we milked the cow, collected the eggs, and fed the animals. The dishes had to be washed after each meal and the scraps went to our hog. We were pioneers on the move, longing and hoping for a better land. We trekked over vast barren prairie where scarcely a tree could be seen anywhere. There didn't seem to be any other folks around but us.*
>
> *The weather was usually sunny by day and cool by night. I remember it raining at least one day. The fences and cattle gates were in place. Animal skeleton heads on the tall poles showed us where the cattle gates were. They could be seen from far distances* (Tena Friesen, pp. 47-49).

Thirteen-year-old Elizabeth reported a more mature version of the same move:

> *Dad came home in late August and announced, "We're moving to Duchess!" He'd found a place. Oh, we rebelled! No way did we want to go south! We wanted to go north where there was no irrigating! Never was I going to be a Rosemaryian! But Dad was stronger, so with wagon and horses hooked to a hayrack with all our earthly possessions on board, we started out.... A cow was tied behind, a pig and chickens crated, we headed once again for a new start. The chickens laid their daily egg. The cow gave us milk. It was a Gypsy sort of life. It took us a week, but we made it.*

> *A certain Mr. Neeb, a retired man, had six fat horses which he let Dad borrow. They were the ones we traveled to Duchess with. We also had a heifer calf, and a yearling.*
>
> *The first day, shortly after we started out, the wagon broke, and it took some time to fix it. We got as far as Bergens south of us in another school district. There we stayed night, sleeping on their floor. It seemed Dad knew people all along the route he chose.*
>
> *At one place we got there quite late. He talked with the boss, and Jake and I were locked in an empty granary for the night. We were each given a blanket and told to sleep there. Well, what to do but just that. We rolled in the blanket and laid on the floor and slept, woke up when the sun was peeking through the cracks and the others were up and opened the door.*
>
> *Another place we stopped, it was afternoon already and Dad sent me in to ask if the lady would cook us some eggs.... The couple were so very old. They had had their meal already and the fire was out, but they had a few sticks there by the stove and proceeded to cook us eggs. I was so embarrassed. I'd rather not had the eggs. People were so hospitable....*
>
> *I can't imagine how hard that trip was on Mom. The cookstove was set up on the wagon so she could cook and bake on it. Annie was a four-month-old baby, that made it nine children. I the oldest was barely thirteen.*
>
> *We traveled to Hutton, Pollockville, and to the Red Deer River. We crossed Matziwan Creek and passed the William's farms, across Jack Garret's lease and to our farm on the then No.1 Highway* (p. 19).

Three-year-old Melita's unforgettable memory from that trip was how fascinated she was by a small hole in the floor of the wagon. She watched the grass and ground whiz by beneath.

Then she discovered that, by applying some force, she could put her foot down through this hole. But, to her consternation, she couldn't pull it back up again! After jerking and pulling, it finally came out, minus the shoe which fell to the ground below. The wagon continued its way. Dismayed at her loss, she was afraid to tell anyone. Shoes were scarce, and she was devastated, knowing that it was lost forever.

The trip involved a total of eight days, counting the day of departure, August 25, and the day of arrival which was September 1, 1933. They covered a total of about 120 miles. The rack they traveled on was a regular 8ft. x 16ft. hay rack. The canopy and benches were just small, big enough to cover mother and baby and the crib. A straw mattress was laid across the top of the chicken crate for the whole family to sleep on. It rained one night and the family, except the baby, got soaked

Starting Over Again

Once again, the family had to make the many adjustments to a new home, a new way of farming, a new community, a new school, a new church, and new friends. By this time, they had made so many moves that they were quite amenable to change. Tena, after what she and her family had been through, was favorably impressed with the new living situation. She wrote:

> *It was very good CPR land with a small weather-beaten cottage and a couple other buildings on it. There was a small grey chicken coop, a straw barn, and a grey outhouse* (p. 45).
>
> *This new home had three bedrooms, one large kitchen and living room combined, and an open veranda running the full length of this old grey-white cottage. Two well-worn wooden steps were attached to the middle of the veranda and in front of the door. They creaked loudly each time anybody stepped on them.*
>
> *We all gave the house an instant inspection. The walls were plastered over slats. Big cracks and holes appeared in the corners and across the walls and ceiling. A trap door led into a full-sized attic that had only a partial floor. Another trap door led into a dirt cellar, and the floors were rough splintered boards, but I was happy about our move and immediately dreamed of how I could make it look better.*
>
> *There was a deep wood-cased well about twenty paces from the front door. On a gate above the well hung a tin pail on a rope. The water supply seemed adequate for now. I drew some water and the rope slipped out of my hand sending the*

> *tin pail to the bottom of the well. There was a lot of fuss made over that. Jake and my father had to fetch it which was not an easy task. Pails were scarce in those days and after its retrieval the rope was permanently secured to a pole to prevent it from happening again...* (pp. 50, 51).

Elizabeth recalls:

> *We arrived at our CPR house September 1, in the late afternoon. We hastily set up housekeeping and all slept in a house that night.... Here we were at Duchess.... It was a half section of land. I think Dad worked out. Mom and the oldest children picked potatoes for Mervin Stanton and took potatoes in payment. That's how we got our potatoes for the winter. We somehow got other vegetables too.*
>
> *For fuel, Dad dug coal in John Ware Coulee, and we hauled wood from the Red Deer River. The quality of the coal was quite poor. Our parents said the coal kept us warm four times: when digging it, in carrying it to the stove, from its warmth when burning, and in carrying out the ashes.... With irrigation Mom could again raise a good garden and we were never short on vegetables. She had big gardens and always with flowers.*
>
> *We went two-and one-half miles to West Duchess School. Mr. L. C. Kadey was our teacher. We liked him okay.... We walked most of the time or drove with horses when the weather was not good. I had grades six and seven in this school.*
>
> *Susan Lily was born on this farm on March 30, 1935. When we came home from the neighbors, we had a baby girl. We kids named her Susanna Lily. Edward John and Martha Marie were born in Bassano Hospital on April 22, 1936, and October 12, 1937.... In March 1936, I started to work for Corny and Lois Siemens when their daughter, Wilda, was born. When Mom went to the hospital for Ed's birth, brother Jake came to get me, meeting me with a big smile and I greeted him with a "How does it feel to have a brother?" It was always so disappointing that he didn't get a brother, now he had one* (p. 20).

Helen remembers her dad had gotten into an argument, with a man on the threshing crew at a neighbor's place, and how he came home frustrated. He was wearing a black hat that had a few holes in it. The story she remembers is that someone got it and threw it up into the air for a target and someone else shot at it.

About the new farm, Helen recalls:

> *This CPR farm had a large slough on it. We waded and played in it, just on the edge, further in it was deep. The older ones would swim the horses in it after a day's work. The duck hunters asked permission to shoot ducks. We girls would sometimes go along, hide behind willows with them and watch the hunters shoot, and then we girls would run to retrieve the dead ducks. I thought one of the young hunters looked like King George. I asked him if he was King George or King George's brother. Those hunters got a big bang out of that. I can still see them laughing.*

Another New School

The West Duchess School was a one-roomed schoolhouse with one teacher, Mr. Kadey in charge, offering grades one to ten,. It was painted white and trimmed in green.

It had a porch entrance which led into a short hallway before the main classroom. The boys cloakroom was on the right side of the hall, and the girls on the left.

There were about forty desks of differing sizes arranged according to grade in the classroom. The desks had a drawer for books under the seat and a shelf under the sloping table. On top there was an inkwell and a groove in which to place the straight pen and pencil. A large teacher's desk faced the student's desks at the front. Large blackboards hung across the front and opposite the east side windows. Near the front there was a bookcase with about twenty library books in it.

At the back of the room was the big black potbellied stove. Near it was the coal pail which doubled as the trash can. A dried pattern of blue ink splattered on the ceiling above the stove bore witness to what happens when a bottle of ink is left on the stove to thaw out for too long. A water fountain stood on a stand to the side at the back as well.

Outside in the school yard there was a flagpole, a playground with a teeter totter and swing set, a cistern with a pump on it, a place for school gardens, a ball field, a horse barn, and a small white three-roomed teacherage that was draughty and cold in winter.

Tena joined her four older siblings in entering their new school in September 1933. She recounts some of the highlights of school days there:

> *Everyday five large lunch pails, usually they were empty syrup or lard pails with a tin lid and handle, had to be filled with school lunches. Most of the time we took sandwiches with homemade "mullah gushy honey" which was two bread slices with a thick cream and sugar mix spread between. I do not remember ever seeing a bologna sandwich while I was in public school. Peanut butter sandwiches were a real rare treat. Often a dill pickle or two from our barrel in the cellar was put into the lunch pails, and they were always appreciated. During lettuce season we received lettuce in between the "gushy honey" sandwiches. When in season, we took a raw carrot and radishes along.*
>
> *Trading sandwiches with other students was interesting. I found out that my sandwiches weren't bad. Many had lard sandwiches which we did also from time to time* (p.116).
>
> *Mr. Kadey was an exceptionally good teacher and an excellent disciplinarian. Students all respected and liked this tall handsome man.... I will always remember the day Mr. Kadey brought his radio to school to let the whole classroom listen to King Edward's abdication speech live from the CBC and discussing it's message and meaning. I'll never forget the way we started each day when my teacher read a chapter or two from the King James Version of the Bible and we all repeated the "Lord's Prayer" before beginning our lessons.... (p. 122).*
>
> *Around 1935 my father built us a nice warm cardboard covered sleigh. It had an opening in front for the reins and a tiny window at the back for a view. It seated six, and sometimes we picked up our neighbor's kids. The food for our horse was placed under the seats. It was a wonderful way to go to school in*

winter because it was so cozy. Sometimes when it was extremely cold, we took warmed up bricks along and a blanket. I thought that this sleigh was great. My father could have made and sold many of its kind, but he never had the material and money he needed to build them.

During the warm weather we took our democrat to school. My father built this two-seater buggy from scrapped pieces.... One day our team got spooked and we had us a real hot dandy runaway team making fast tracks with pounding hoofs and a load of very scared kids on board, and a very frightened driver (myself) trying desperately to gain control. The horses were making one set of tracks going straight ahead, and the democrat came fast behind at an acute angle with the front wheels making another set of tracks, and the back wheels making a third set of tracks, until the front wheels hooked into the fence along the side of the road, and dragged the team to a halt, pulling a part of the fence away in the process.... I think my parents were so happy that nobody was hurt that I never heard of it again (pp. 124, 126).

One very cold winter day I walked to school with my sisters, and on our way home a sudden squall came upon us and we all kind of got lost in the total "white out" blizzard.... We followed a deep drain ditch until we felt that we were as close to home as possible, then we walked along a fence until we reached it. I froze both of my hands and my worried mother put me in a cool room and immersed my hands in coal oil until my hands thawed. It was very painful but there were no adverse effects from the frost bite (p. 125).

I can't say that my next three teachers ever came close to being good educators. They all were young female teachers. Two of them were very cranky and unfair, and the other one was very sweet, everybody loved her, but I can't remember that she ever taught us anything. Her kindness stayed with me.... On the other hand, Miss Day was a real witch! She used to make fun of my mother in front of the class when she taught biology to the boys and compared my mother to animals re:

> *pregnancies, etc. This hurt me a lot. In my opinion this was blatant discrimination against large poor families. The good part is that she only lasted one term. The other teacher was my high school teacher and she yelled and screamed so much that I couldn't concentrate on anything, so I became discouraged and quit school* (p. 123).

By the time Melita entered school, her classmates, who were born at the beginning of the depression in the early thirties, were called "hungry babies" by the older pupils. "Mullah gushy honey" or "Mullingar honey", also called "depression honey," was named after Mullingar, a town about thirty miles northeast of North Battleford. Mennonites in this district get credit for making it. It came in three grades: water and sugar, milk and sugar, or cream and sugar (Information shared by Helen Biehn).

Helen started school in September 1935. She says:

> *I started school with a limited knowledge of the English language, and many warnings from Tena to stay away from the bad boys. I was unable to understand everything Mr. Kadey assigned to us, so had to take grade one over again.*
>
> *One day, he made me stay in after school, to do some work on the blackboard. I was crying because I figured Jake would drive off home without me. Edna Scheuermann and another girl told Mr. Kadey, "Ah, let her go." and he did. Jake had already started, and I had to run to catch up.*
>
> *We children would stop on our way home from school, with the Dyck's and Peltzer's children, and play in the willows along the canal, or play hide and seek in and around an old, abandoned house. Sometimes we spent time drowning the gophers. We would fetch water and pour it down a gopher hole until the gopher came up out of the hole sopping wet and a bit lifeless, and of course that was the end of the gopher.*

Sometimes the Friesen kids would ride a horse, called "Old Pete", to school. With three or four kids on his poor aching back at a time, he didn't seem to mind. He just plodded along in his poky fashion. The horses were kept in the horse barn at school during the day. At noon, the students would give them some oats and a bit of hay.

Sometimes the boys hung around the barn during noons and recesses, bragging, racing their horses, goofing off, telling jokes, (some of them not fit to repeat here) and playing pranks. Helen reports that they tried to smoke horse manure. Obviously, it wasn't a major scientific breakthrough!

Simply Surviving

Tena describes how this family of nine children survived during those hard times.

> *Our local merchant extended us credit.... Each fall we picked up about twelve one-hundred-pound sacks of flour, a hundred pounds of white sugar, large bags of rolled oats, and all the other necessities like yeast, salt, vinegar, and coal oil etc. All of this was drawn up into our attic by rope for winter storage. When we didn't have the money, we charged and after the harvesting was done, we usually paid for it all.*
>
> *My mother had her ways of making our attic 100% intruder proof. The bugs and mice never bothered our precious food stuffs in our attic. The vegetables were put into our dirt cellar. The carrots, beets and turnips were covered over with dry sand to keep them fresh. The potatoes were put into bins and our cabbage was hung on nails from the ceiling. Our pumpkins went into our attic. Our house outside had to have straw and sod piled around the base, so the hard frost didn't penetrate and freeze our vegetables in our cellar....* (p. 52).

The proximity of the Friesen home to the Trans-Canada Highway, and later to the railroad, made it an oasis where many a transient found shelter for a night or a warm meal to further him on his way. Tena recalls:

> *My mother always gave a transient food and shelter unless she felt insecure, at which time she sent them to our neighbor because there were men there. We were mostly women in our*

house during these happenings, but somehow the transients from all parts of Canada seemed to find our place. Sometimes they put a rock on a fence post to alert others of our place, or they placed a tin can near our gate indicating that our place was a good place to stop over.

Each man came with a personal tragedy that my parents understood. It was a tragedy that my parents could relate to. They showed all who stopped their personal compassion, and we all listened to these men tell their own stories. Some of their stories were very sad. Today we fear such transients because of the problem of chemical abuse in our society, but in those days these men were just desperate men on the road looking for any kind of permanent job. Many were my brother's age. Normally these young men would be helping to run the country and communities, but instead they were sad, lonely, worried men helplessly searching for a better life, as they desperately moved from one temporary job to another.

We particularly looked forward to one travelling peddler in an old beat-up truck to come around every summer to sell his wares. It was like a Vaudeville show without the song and dance. He had potions, liniments, salves, and cure-alls. He had used pots and pans, kettles, sad irons, and live hens in crates. He was an average skinny man with twitchy eyes and parched lips. His hair was sparse and dry. He was also a victim of the times. This was his way of surviving the "Dirty Thirties" (pp 56, 57).

Having Good Times in Bad Times

Although the family was very poor, the children found many creative ways to entertain themselves. Tena writes about some of those fun things:

My father made us a large dugout about 20' x 12' and about a foot deep which was filled with dry sand for us children to play in. It was such nice clean fine sand and children could create the nicest things in it. This is where my sisters and I let our creative imaginations soar. There was enough space for each one of

> *us to be free to create. It was here where I built my ranch, my dream home with many clothes closets and bedrooms, my kind of town, my own road. Green sticks made from green willows were my fence posts, the leafy branches were my trees, flour sack string served as my fence wire, and everything I used was free and within my reach.... I used real water in my ditches....*
>
> *Another good thing for children to have to explore is an old, abandoned car. We had two of them near our house where I played whenever the weather was wet or chilly. It was great fun to take imaginary trips, and I also learned to shift gears and lots of other things about car parts. I liked the soft seats and the windows that I could open and close at will. It was the privacy I liked best of all.*
>
> *During the winter we had cardboard boxes in the house. They served as doll houses, as wagons to travel in, or a place in which to hide. We had marbles and "Snakes and Ladders" to play with. There were dominoes and "Chinese Checkers" and some games like X's and O's to master. We had a patch of ice beside the house and two old pairs of skates which we shared as we all tried to learn to skate. We really did not have warm enough clothes to spend much time outside doing winter fun, but we all had at least a few tries at it. We had a sled and we made snow men....*
>
> *For hobbies we used our imagination, a pair of scissors, some paper, a catalogue, a cardboard box and some home-made flour and water glue. Out of this stuff we made doll houses, farm wagons, furniture, sleighs, animals, and all sorts of wonderful playthings. We all had our turn to learn to sew on our old treadle sewing machine. A charming old pump organ was there for all of us to practice on* (pp. 53-55).

It didn't take a lot of money or expensive electronic toys to have a lot of fun, as Helen recalls:

> *With a bit of imagination, we could think of a lot of things to entertain ourselves. We played house, church, and school. We*

> *played horse. We were horses and used twine string for our reins. We made ourselves pretend cars, with a sunflower head for a steering wheel mounted on a broom stick. We drove all over the world. We made up our own language, just a bunch of gibberish, but we had fun!*
>
> *The Eaton's and Simson Sears Catalogues were a real blessing to us children. We cut out the people, "paper people", we called them. We made furniture for them. We even wrapped them in paper and buried them when they died. After many days we unearthed them to see what they looked like.*
>
> *We played with the little animals too. One day someone brought two baby rabbits in from the field. Melita and I played with these two rabbits. We were so happy, until we put them into two small syrup pails and put the lids on. We just did not realize the terminal consequence.* (A personal letter from my Aunt Helen Biehn).

Horses were an important part of recreation and work. Helen recalls:

> *Dad taught us to ride at an early age. He put me on a horse and said I was to ride it out to the slough and let it drink and then come home again. While it was drinking, I dropped the halter rope. Good thing the water wasn't very deep. I slid off into the water to fetch the rope but couldn't get on him again. So, I led him home.*

Watching the older people work also was entertaining to the younger ones. While the mother and older girls were milking the cows out in the yard, the young ones would come around with a cup and take turns getting the cup filled with the foaming milk direct from the cow's teat and drink it on the spot. What a treat!

Sometimes Elizabeth would entertain the younger ones with her story telling. This was often done outside in the evenings. They would gather around her, and she would start her story and make it up as she went along. The story would go on until bedtime. Sometimes it would continue for many days.

Sometimes the parents would both go away to visit someone for a while and leave the children home alone. They would play games or sit and talk. Helen remembers one time they were discussing "love." They decided they would rather live in an old shack and have love, than to live in a mansion and not have love.

Christmas always sparks excitement and hope in the heart of a child that not even the darkest days of the Depression nor deepest poverty can snuff out. Tena remembers some of those times:

> *Christmas time in our community... was always a very busy time. The preparations began in November and lasted well past the New Year.... Teachers were judged by their performance in producing our stage show, and the students all had their parts to practice and learn....*
>
> *Shopping for the annual treats of nuts, candy and easy-to-peel oranges was done about a week before Christmas Day. Other goodies like the silver balls, colored cookie decorations, cake flavors, and cake coloring were all on the shopping list.*
>
> *Farmers...came in their wagons and horse-drawn sleighs laden with home-made butter, eggs, and a variety of farm produce all to be bartered for the things on their shopping list from the local General Store. These items became a part of the store's stock or went to other retailers or wholesalers in the city.*
>
> *My earliest recollections of Christmas at home are the sounds of big spinning tops making music early on Christmas morning before anybody was up but us kids. There was a pink comb in a delicate pink silk case with a pink tassel on my plate and there was a doll for each one of us girls. They were called." Sunshine Susie" or." Raggedy Ann" dolls. I only ever had two store-bought dolls and one was a very tiny porcelain baby doll in a tiny basket. When it got broken, I never played with dolls again (p. 136).*
>
> *We had real green trees at our place.... My parents made home-made tallow candles and the clasps, which held them to the branches, were made from tin lids and wooden clothes pins.*

We had a few ready-made candle holders just so we knew that they existed.

The lighting of these candles was done under the strictest supervision, and then carefully watched until they were burned down, and it was done on Christmas Eve and Christmas Day only. It was very dangerous, so we only got to enjoy them shine for a very short time. You can imagine the anticipation it created before this scene around our tree could take place.

Often the tree decorations were made from strung up colored popcorn, or from crepe paper streamers. It was a wonderful moment to remember, and then it was all over until another Christmas came around.

It was difficult to go to sleep on Christmas Eve and miss Santa Claus. At our place he left our gifts on dinner plates on the table or in flour sacks tied to our beds.

We were always up early on Christmas morning and had great expectations. There was always something for everybody. Sometimes it was just one coloring book, a box of crayons, a handful of nuts, and a few hard candies, but we were happy that there was something. To find an easy-to-peel orange or an apple was a real big treat. Some years were more generous than others. Once I remember getting a small red wagon and another time, we all got a small sleigh which we all had to share.

Our Christmas concerts were held in the evening. Families came from far to our school in open sleighs. Nobody stayed at home that night. Even the tiny babies came along. All the class sat in the front rows; the mothers sat near the heater with the small children.... The school was packed with the community folk. All the pupils took part in the choir.... The bitter cold weather outside and "Good King Wenceslas" and "The Weather Outside Is Frightful" all seemed very fitting for the occasion.... Our traditional carols... were always sung with gusto.... But "Silent Night, Holy Night" was very special and was the last carol to be sung.

Then Santa Claus in his red and white suit came jingling up the side aisle to the front of the stage with a huge sack full of goodies for all the children present that night. He came with a jolly "Ho! Ho! Ho!" and a big belly that shook just like a bowl of jelly, and the excited children could be heard squealing with delight as their names were called to come and fetch their brown bags full of Christmas goodies. In that bag were hard candies, oranges, apples, peanuts, walnuts, other nuts, and something of surprise.

The long trip home in the cold somehow didn't seem quite so long because everybody was so happy (pp.136-143).

A "Sign of the Times"

Those difficult times caused a lot of people to think about the ultimate questions. Is there really a God? If so, why does He allow this to happen to us? Is God punishing us for something, or for some mysterious reason? Is this one of the calamities predicted in the Bible? Is the end of the world near? People pondered and talked and formed their own opinions, but no one understood. These were unusual times, and strange things happened. Some called them "signs of the times." Tena describes one of these strange phenomena in the sky:

One evening around eleven p.m. my mother woke us up to come and witness a rare phenomenon outside. The whole earth and sky were enveloped in a rosy pink to rouge hue. Three crosses of white were where the moon should be with the large cross in the middle. It was a very still evening, and there was an air of mystery and an eerie strange feeling. There was no breeze and it felt as if we were about to experience an earthquake. I will always remember it because my mother said it was a message from God giving us a sign to prepare for the great bloodshed to come.

I saw many heavenly phenomena like bursting fireballs, shooting stars, and some exceptionally bright stars, but I had never ever seen such a burning sight and I have not seen anything like it since. This happened during the mid-thirties. I remember that my pink shadow was long and thin and that the reddish hue over the whole earth and sky lasted for hours. Was it a bad omen? Or was it just a coincidence that later World War Two was declared and that terrible bloodshed followed (p. 128)?

Divine Drawing

Elizabeth reminisces about her spiritual development during those next few years:

At first, we went to the General Conference Mennonite Church in Rosemary. Our attendance was rather sporadic, but we did get some Sunday school. In our school they started a Saturday school in winter where we learned German. We had a good teacher, and I would say Sunday school experience was good. Later I also went to choir practice often walking seven miles one way. I had a strong desire for the good things, church, Sunday school, choir, Bible study, etc. I delighted in evenings of singing, music, and recitations. The Christian youngfolks of Rosemary entertained them-selves this way when they got together Sunday afternoons or evenings, especially in winter.

It was so far and transportation so meager, I seldom got to go. I often wonder why it was so difficult for me when I wanted so bad to be where the good things were, while others had all the opportunities and didn't seem to appreciate them.... It was seven miles and I walked and sometimes it was cold. When I'd get back Mom would be up and Jake sometimes and we'd have a cup of hot postum and talk.... Later in life I asked Mom how she felt when I'd just walk off seven or eight miles by myself to church or choir practice etc. She said, "I could see you wanted the good things, and I couldn't say anything."

One Sunday in the month, the church would have a program of music, songs, and recitations. I often recited.

The youngfolks in our area often did things I didn't enjoy, so my going with them petered out. We encountered the Duchess Mennonite Church. The people were very good to us. At fifteen I started to work out, not steady, just here and there for a month at a time for people who were expecting babies, or to pay off

Dad's bills. In between I worked at home. I went more and more to the Duchess church.

In 1937 we had our first Summer Bible School. Mervin Stanton came to see if any of us wanted to come. I wanted to ever so bad, but thought I was too old, but he encouraged me, said it was for ages four to eighteen. I wasn't quite seventeen, so I qualified. Mervin Stanton took us faithfully for two weeks. We knew no English Bible, but we learned.

We had no Bibles and no money to get them with, even though they were only twenty-five cents each. One afternoon a man came and gave us a dollar for a bag of carrots. How were we going to spend this dollar among so many needs? Mom said, "I think Elizabeth will agree it should go for Bibles." I did, and we got four, our first English Bibles.

At the age of twelve I was carefree as to my spiritual life. When we died, we went to heaven, I was sure! My girlfriend wasn't so sure. "How do you know?" she asked. I just knew. It could have been a difference in teaching as they were Brethren and Mom was General Conference.

Then one day a Brethren minister, a stranger to us kids at least, came to visit at our home. Dad and he called us children in and had a little meeting with us. He asked me several questions I couldn't answer nor understand, didn't know what he was talking about. I can still see his piercing blue eyes; he was a white-haired man. I was very confused. He asked Dad some questions. Dad wasn't the one who taught us, so he didn't know, said his wife did the teaching.... I was a confused girl when he was done with us. To this day, I don't thank him. God is love and He loved me, a twelve-year-old girl, Mom believed that.

I think I was fourteen or fifteen when we attended some meetings in Duchess Mennonite Church, and I heard for the first time in an understandable way that we needed to accept Jesus as our Savior in our hearts. Someone invited me to go forward. I wanted to ever so bad, but Dad was in the audience, and I was afraid. At age sixteen I made public my commitment.

> *At the time of Summer Bible School, I had a strong urge, I could wait no longer, I had to be baptized. That fall on October 28, 1937, I was baptized along with two others, Ruth Stanton, and Eldon Spicer, by Bishop N.E. Roth of Tofield. The text was "Wist ye not that I must be about my Father's business?" Lu. 2:49. One of the songs was "O Happy Day!" It was a happy day!*
>
> *In those days we had three weeks Winter Bible School (for adults) at the local churches. I went two winters in Duchess. It was a wonderful experience, a wonderful time* (pp. 20, 21).

Since the German Mennonites used the high German in their worship and Sunday school services, the younger Friesen children had little incentive to go to church or Sunday school. When Elizabeth started to attend the Duchess Mennonite Church where everything was in English, the younger children were more than glad to go along. They also enjoyed the Summer Bible School there. It was far to church, so they didn't get there every Sunday. Sometimes they rode horses.

Whereas, the Mennonites that came from Russia had a Dutch/German/Russian background, the Duchess Mennonite Church was established by Mennonite pioneers who came from the English-speaking Mennonites of Pennsylvania and other parts of the USA and Ontario, Canada. Theirs was a Swiss/German/North American background.

Hence, although, as Anabaptists, their theological understandings were compatible, their cultures and histories were quite different.

Through the decades, as both streams accommodated to the cultural setting in North America, these two streams came together and merged in 2002. The Mennonite Church and the General Conference Mennonite denominations joined together, forming "The Mennonite Church" in the USA, and "Mennonite Church Canada" in Canada.

Surviving Exploitation of Child Labor

Irrigated farming was more labor intensive, and the children were getting bigger, so their parents expected them to carry more of the burden. Tena comments on those times.

A lot of classes were missed every spring because we had to help get the crops and garden into the ground. Our daily chores had to be done twice a day like the milking and the hauling of water. We learned early in life to distinguish the weeds from the good plants. We sat on dusty harrows and ploughs to add weight so the soil would get a good workout. We took turns on the seeders, and we piled onto the large land floats to level the land and make it smooth before planting.... There was always lots of work to be done... so we had only a little time each evening for play before going to bed (p. 127).

My father was often away from home. He'd get up early, have his breakfast, and leave only to return after all the chores were done in the evening. Once the plowing and seeding were done, that was his daily routine until harvesting started. He never ever had any kind of special line of work. His jobs were where he could get them.... Farming was not the kind of work that my father was best at....

While he was away doing odd jobs for a pittance... we were left to fend for ourselves. Once spring seeding was done it was mostly left to the rest of the family to bring it to fruition. We did it all; the chores, the irrigating, the weeding, the cultivating, and the canning and gathering up of the produce in the fall. Whenever we couldn't handle a problem, he had to deal with it. We learned early in life to do all our tasks without prodding (pp. 57, 58).

We all took our turn hauling water up from the well on a very slippery rope to keep our barrel in the kitchen full, and to water the cattle. Once a day we filled all our vessels full of fresh water and carried out the dirty water. Most of the time the girls did this job after school. During the winter it would splash over and turn our skirts into ice. It was a nasty job in the biting cold weather and blowing snow.... There was a wooden trough near the well beside the barnyard fence so the cattle could poke their heads through it for a drink. The trough had to be chopped free from ice during the freezing months. Sometimes it was so cold

> *we had to bring hot water from the house to warm it up for the cattle* (p. 66).

Elizabeth recounts her bitter experiences with overwork:

> *We worked very hard at home.... I resented being a girl. If I had to work like a man, why wasn't I a man? Yet Jake had it worse. He was still a boy, but he had to work like a man.*
>
> *I remember my last ditch. I think Jake was working away and I was helping get the crop seeded and making ditches for irrigating. Work was done with horses. The field ditches were not so bad, but then came cleaning the head ditches, that was bad. When that was done to Dad's satisfaction, he wanted us to cut a ditch through raw prairie with the ditcher.*
>
> *The horses and I were already "done for." We just couldn't, just couldn't. We didn't care anymore. I thought "You can hit us with a fencepost, and I wouldn't care!" We couldn't respond anymore. We were done for. I left the lines go slack and the horses headed for home, and I followed as best I could. In my mind it was going around, "My last ditch! Never again! I don't care what you do, I can't anymore, never again, my last ditch!" The horses and I gave up and dragged home, not a word was said. Dad followed without a word. That was my last ditch.*
>
> *I was just done for. I felt it all over my body. I had promised Siemens I'd work for them for two weeks in June to help get ready for Conference and I did. They were pleased and asked if I'd stay for the rest of the summer.... By August I was so bad I couldn't work anymore. I didn't care what happened, but I didn't want to go home. The doctor said it was my kidneys. Siemens, in their great kindness and understanding, said if I could do light work like wash dishes, etc. I could stay on for my board. I did that until harvest was finished, then I came home.*
>
> *It was a real miserable time. I accepted my lot in life and had peace. I remember that peace. Life was sort of hopeless with no future, but I had peace, peace in the midst of my storm. My friends felt sorry for me for now no one would ever marry me.*

> *Siemens paid me my wages and I got four dresses and one each for each of my sisters. I took the bus to Medicine Hat, did my shopping there and visited a doctor. He told me to go home and go to bed.... That was in the spring and summer of 1938* (p. 22).

Helen understandingly explained that "those ditches were made with a Martin ditcher. It would wear Samson out on sod" (referring to "Samson," the Biblical superhero). It seems Elizabeth suffered a physical and emotional breakdown due to abusing her body through overwork when she was still too young. She was a fast grower and reached her full height at age fourteen. Because she was big for her age and firstborn, her father put big demands on her which she tried to meet, but it was too much, and she suffered the effects for the rest of her life.

After this breakdown, she received a lot of comfort and help from a local Christian "chiropractor", Mr. Ed Porter of Duchess, who helped to get her going again. She was eternally grateful to him.

Jake didn't fare any better. From age twelve through fourteen, he only got to school two or three days a week, because his dad piled so many duties on him. He struggled to make the grades. When he did attend, he used recesses and noon hours to catch up.

In the spring season, he used to get up at four o'clock in the morning and plow until seven, then rush in and eat a bite of breakfast, and walk three miles to school. In the evening he would walk home and plow until dark which could be past ten at night at that time of year. Of course, the plowing was still done by horse as they had no tractor in those days. He had to repeat grade five.

Jake was paralyzed in an accident when he was lifting a seed drill. The drill fell off its block and wrenched his back. They took him to Ed Porter, the chiropractor, but he sent him to the doctor in Brooks. The physician there said I can't help him, take him to Ed Porter. So, he was brought back.

Ed bowed his head and prayed, then he treated him. Within three days Jake was able to walk again. But the injury left a lifelong effect. A nerve was pinched in such a way that it affected his heartbeat. From time to time, he had to seek the help of chiropractors.

In the summer when he was thirteen years of age, Jake was sent to rake hay for Jack Garret.

They used a dump rake in those days. It was a device that had two large wheels about ten or twelve feet apart joined by an axle. At the center of this axle was a wooden tongue protruding forward to which two horses were hitched. On top of this tongue was a seat for the operator. Behind was a row the full width of the rake of large, curved C-shaped iron teeth fastened at the top. They were spaced about six inches apart. They were lifted or lowered by a lever which the operator controlled from the seat.

When the horses pulled this contraption across a mown hay field the operator would lower the teeth and they would slide along the ground, scoop up the hay, and roll it together until the rake was about full. Then the operator would lift the teeth with the lever and all the bunched hay would remain behind. This operation would be repeated until all the hay in the field was in bunches or rows. It was hard work and required a strong arm.

This day as the thirteen-year-old Jake was raking, the wooden tongue came apart. So, he tied it up with a halter shank and took it home and took another rake. This one had a faulty tongue as well, but it was nailed together. He asked the boss about it, but the boss said it would be okay, so he took it to the field and continued his work. But after a while the tongue suddenly broke off and the seat tipped forward, dumping the boy onto the ground behind the horses but in front of the rake. The horses kept on going, rolling the boy along on the ground with the gathering hay! Jake passed out.

He woke up under a pile of hay in a head ditch near the canal, near to where he had been working. Bruised and sore, he was able to get up and walk to the homestead. But a neighbor working about a quarter of a mile away had gotten to the boss before him and reported that he had seen the boy stand up and beat the horses. So, the boss sent Jake back to the field to bring the horses home. Jake tried but he couldn't make it. Finally, the boss came and took the horses home and told Jake to sit until he would come back with the car to get him. When he was brought to the house, Jake vomited and couldn't eat. So, Jack Garret took him home.

Jake quit school on his fifteenth birthday and went to work out for Mr. Corny Krause at Rosemary in 1937. His dad came and collected all his wages. According to the law and common practice, it was right for a child, under twenty-one years of age, to bring his wages home to his parents.

Intimations of Romance

As is often the case, when we are in our deepest darkest valley, God has something new and exciting just over the next hill. So, it was in the life of the young Elizabeth. She recounts her story:

> *In the spring of '38 we were getting a new neighbor. Dad was always finding things out and said the new neighbor was moving in now and was getting his wife and children after the crop was in. He was from Saskatchewan.*
>
> *One day I was tidying up in the house after the kids had left for school. Mom and I noticed a man moving; wagon loaded with stuff, cow tied behind, a couple of horses and a saddle horse and a colt alongside, and the man walking. We wondered, "Is this the new neighbor?" I leaned on the window and watched, all sorts of thoughts going through my mind; will his wife and I be friends? I longed very much for a real friend; one I could share with. I watched till he turned the corner going north and till he was out of sight. We were assured it was him. I went back to work.*
>
> *One Saturday, the neighbor lady, Mrs. Peltzer, was sick and asked if I would come and wash their floors. I did. While I was there this new neighbor came and wanted Mr. Peltzer who was out in the field attending a cow. It was the first-time meeting. His accent was heavy, and I had trouble understanding. In me arose a strong determination, here's a man I'm going to understand. I was surprised at myself. I had never acted like this before. I couldn't understand myself. The Peltzer girls were outside... They were so excited. They told me he was a bachelor. Oh boy! I thought, "He'll never look at me again!"*
>
> *One day Dad was going to ride along to town with him, and he drove up to the house. I peeked from behind the curtain for a better look.*
>
> *Then I went to Corny Siemens to work. Sundays, when I came home, my sisters could talk of nothing else but "the Dane." One Sunday the Siemens decided to visit my folks. We all went.*

We were visiting in the house when the Dane came. After a bit, they brought him in for lunch and we were introduced. I served him a drink, and Siemens noticed how pleased he looked. They couldn't believe it was the first time we really met. They thought, "There is something between them."

That night I dreamed about him, but when I awoke, I thought, "No way am I going to think such stuff, and I set my mind to forget that dream and I did thoroughly and permanently. To this day I can't recall what it was.

After I came home from Siemens, we had threshers. He was on the crew. I observed covertly and said to Mom, "What a neck!" Later one evening he came for a visit. Dad wasn't home. All the kids, Mom, and I visited together. Then Mom sent the kids to bed, and we visited. Had a nice time. When he left, I saw him to the door and said, "Come again!" And he said, "I will." Later he told me he was glad Dad wasn't home.

7

Surviving Homelessness

> *But Moses fled from Pharaoh and went to live in Midian.... Moses agreed to stay with the man, who gave his daughter Zipporah to Moses in marriage.* – Exodus 2:15, 21 NIV.

Things didn't go well on the Friesen farm. There were harvests but there was no market for the produce. The Depression continued its strangle hold on the economic throats of the struggling farmers. The Friesen family found they were getting poorer and poorer. Tena gives some examples:

> *We didn't have enough bedding. Our winter clothes were terribly inadequate. Our shoes were fixed so many times over by my father that to be walking on sharp nails on bloody feet was not unusual. Our diet from March to late spring consisted of a lot of bread and milk. My mother had about a hundred and one recipes for bread dough and each one was good* (p. 92).
>
> *All of us wore hand-me-downs until they were completely worn out.... Many times, our coats weren't warm enough and my mother stitched a piece of used chamois from an old used coat, or she sewed an extra layer of padded cloth in the back area to make it warmer. She saved all bits of old wool so she could keep our mittens in good repair. We didn't have sweaters to keep us warm. With so many young children close together she was always busy knitting and mending things for all her children* (p. 93).

How to keep warm and cook was a major concern.... Fuel had to be gathered by hand before the cold weather set in. It was a tradition... for our family to hitch a team of horses to a hayrack, another team to our wagon, pack food and drinks, and head out to the Red Deer River for our wood, and to the John Ware Coulee for our coal. This was a family affair. The women gathered the loose dry wood all day, and neatly and carefully stacked it high on the hayrack until not another piece of wood could be put onto it anywhere....

The men would head for the old coal mine shafts in the John Ware Coulee to fetch our free coal.... Hauling coal is very hard work and digging for it with a hand shovel was not an easy task, but we scraped the old coal beds of all its best coal.... Often the lumps I carried were so heavy they would bring me down on my knees several times before I got help to get it loaded into the wagon.... Usually, we made two or more trips before we had what we needed to see us through a severe winter.

When we got these loads home the wood had to be unloaded and chopped into proper lengths before it all was neatly stacked away in the woodshed. All the coal had to be unloaded into the coal bin in the shed.

Once our wagon wheel broke just as we were about to leave. We stayed all night while the men repaired it by the light of the moon and a coal oil lantern. It was pure adventure for children but not so for my parents (pp. 94, 95).

Sometimes we were just too poor to replace our worn dresses in the spring and that is when it became rough. Sometimes we just didn't have a dress to wear, and we had to stay home or take turns with one dress. One day my sister went and the next day the other sister wore the same dress to school while the first sister stayed home (p. 114).

The Depression was flour sack dresses, flour sack bedding, flour sack towels, flour sack curtains, and flour sack mattress covers.... I would save all the pennies that I earned, and when I had enough, I sent away for bleached flour sacks and... sugar sacks. For about $1.40 I got twenty-four flour sacks, and for

> *$2.00 I got twelve large sugar sacks. It was the only gift I could give my mother. It also made me feel very good* (p. 102).
>
> *The Depression meant shopping and getting an education from the T. Eaton catalogue without spending any money, and never sending away for anything. My imagination was a wonderful thing; it kept my dreams alive* (p. 102).
>
> *For many years we had the bed frames but no real mattresses. We had mattresses made from large flour sacks sewn together into double bed-sized bags. Each bag was filled with lots of fresh golden straw until it formed a small mountain on the bed. We carried the straw in small bags into the house to fill the larger ones and changed the straw whenever needed except during the worst cold in winter. These mattresses were hygienically much cleaner than real ones because there were wet beds, and it was easy to change.*
>
> *These mattresses were most uncomfortable because the bed springs sagged deep in the middle. Nobody wanted to sleep all "squished" in the valley in the middle, but we took our turns just the same. The good thing about straw mattresses is that it was easy to replace the old with new straw from the... stacks outside.... There is something very pleasant about that first night's smell of the fresh clean straw whenever we changed it* (pp. 150, 151).

Money was hard to get. Friesens traded a cow and her twin calves for twenty-five bushels of wheat. Cows sold for nine dollars a head. They got forty-nine cents for a can of cream, and thirty-eight cents for a bushel of wheat if they could sell it. The children tried to earn a little pocket money by hunting gophers, magpies, and crows, and their eggs. In government bounties, gopher tails brought a penny for a pair, crow or magpie feet brought two pennies for a pair, and their eggs were five cents.

They collected beer and pop bottles and cashed them in for pennies. In winter Jake and some of his sisters learned to trap fur bearing animals such as skunk and weasels, but they only had four traps and couldn't afford more, so their earnings were limited. Sometimes they were blessed with a job with a neighbor baby-sitting, picking potatoes, doing chores, scrubbing floors, house cleaning, or whatever else that was needed. The money they earned was put to good use in meeting the needs of the family.

Helen remembers that the family did receive government relief from time to time for several years. The Royal Canadian Mounted Police (R.C.M.P.) administered the relief by issuing a food coupon once a month. It was worth ten dollars for a family and five dollars for a single person living alone. There were frequent investigations to see that it was needed. When the girls would see the police officer coming, they would inform the rest and dance on the spot clapping their hands and say, "Goody! Goody! We will get something to eat!" They did receive help from kind neighbors and the local church in the form of used clothes, vegetables, and other food items.

Every fall MCC would send them a gunny sack or two of used clothing. One fall they got a whole sack of neck ties! How useful for a family of nine girls facing a cold winter! If the used dresses didn't fit, their mother would remake them to fit the girls. But what could one do with neck ties? Tena reports that her folks used to send surplus garden produce by Greyhound Bus service to Calgary for "the poor folk" there. Apparently, it was distributed under the direction of the Red Cross. Then one day they received a surprise. Tena relates:

> *The Greyhound bus passed our place every morning and every evening. On a nice warm day, my sisters and I waited near the highway just so we could wave as it passed. The driver always waved and tooted his horn, and the passengers also smiled and waved back much to our delight. I wonder what thoughts must have gone through the driver's mind when he saw poor barefoot, raggedly dressed, straight-haired, squinty-eyed little girls waving frantically, waiting to be noticed. Our faces were often dirty and our noses runny, but these drivers were very aware of world conditions during the Great Depression....*
>
> *One day the bus stopped. It was in the early fall. The driver got out, opened the bottom compartment of the bus, and unloaded a large box of stuff plus several sacks full of goodies. He told us it came from Calgary and that it was ours to keep. Well, that caused a big stir. It had never happened to us before. We ran to the house to get our mother. My mother and older*

sisters brought all of it into the house. I was about eight or nine years old.

When they opened the big box there were several nice warm blankets, some winter boots and coats, some warm mittens, caps, and hand muffs. There were dresses; some of them were very silky and pretty. We had nice dresses for Christmas that year! There must have been some Christmas gifts as well, as we weren't allowed to see some of the contents. These goodies were taken up to our attic and hidden away in a place where we were not allowed to go and peek (pp. 91, 92).

Homeless Again

The whole family worked and scrimped and saved and pulled together, but they were fighting a losing battle. The Great Depression relentlessly wore them down and defeated them. There was no money to pay their obligations, and once again Jacob Friesen lost his farm, and in November 1938, was forced to move his big family out of their home. But this time they had no place to go, and winter was upon them.

Their new neighbor, Jens Hansen, was living in his five-room house by himself. Jacob went over to inquire if it would be possible to find shelter there for his family. Helen and Melita went along and ate frozen crab apples from Jens's trees while their father was inside talking. Jens agreed to give the family shelter for the winter if they would cook for him.

There wasn't much choice, so the Friesen family, with twelve children, moved in. For sure, the lonely bachelor's private lifestyle was drastically altered. In the spring, they decided to continue the arrangement with Friesens farming half of the land.

The younger Friesen girls adored Jens. He was always nice to them and tolerated them when they hung around him. Helen recalls: "I remember playing 'telephone', we all sat in a circle with Elizabeth and Jens sitting together. I'm not sure how it happened, but Elizabeth enjoyed herself."

The couple sometimes tried to get away for a little privacy just to be alone together, but the little girls would always search for the couple until they found them, then they would surround them, and Jens would play with them.

They also admired the way he treated his horses. Helen says, one evening, after a busy day of harvesting at the Friesen farm, they were at the end of the lane. Jens left his white riding horse, Nancy, loose and clapped his hands and she took off home at a nice trot. She marveled that the horse would really go home. Jens had to drive his work horses home later. Nancy was a smart horse. She could open a prairie gate with her teeth.

Corny Siemens recorded his observations:

> *Then in 1939, Elizabeth worked for us again.... For some odd reason, when I would come in from the field in the evening, there would be a horse tied to the fence. A nice young stranger would be there. Didn't seem to be too interested in our company? We were glad to have him, he seemed so nice, but oh, so shy!*
>
> *Then he started to come to church. He had no car; we could see no horse. But we found out he left it tied behind the hotel, the only place that had accommodations for that. Of course, our way home went right past where it was. Once we knew, we rejoiced that he took that effort to come. It looked good! We had watched all this for some time, but it was kept a secret. Of course, we enjoyed... to see this slowly unfold.* (A speech on Jens and Elizabeth's fortieth anniversary celebration).

Women must have been much the same then as they are purported to be now. It is often what the young man drives that attracts the girl. Years later someone asked Jens: "What did you do to catch Elizabeth's attention?" He replied: "She liked my white horse!"

Jens and Elizabeth were obviously interested in each other before this house-sharing arrangement was made. Besides normal human compassion for the destitute, this interest must have had something to do with softening Jens's heart to welcome this significant intrusion into his private home.

The arrangement did bring some complications. Jacob's well-meaning German Mennonite friends at Rosemary warned him of the most terrible consequences that would likely result if he allowed the thirty-four-year-old Dane to marry his eighteen-year-old daughter. Then he would work on his wife's fears. In those days it was unthinkable for a Mennonite to marry a person of another denomination, and it was equally unthinkable for a German to marry a person of another ethnic origin.

Therefore, the parents did what all concerned parents feel they should do. They tried to stop this growing romance in the bud stage. Jacob approached his daughter and informed her: "You can't get married without my permission!" To this declaration, the now eighteen-year-old Elizabeth replied, "Then I'll wait until I'm twenty-one!" On another occasion, while Jacob was driving to town with Jens he very correctly and courageously did the fatherly thing and informed Jens that there was no way that he could marry his daughter. Jens replied calmly; "If she wants to, I'm not going to ask you!"

So much for the protocol! Jens declared his love to the sweet Elizabeth, and she responded in the appropriate positive manner, and their engagement was sealed on March 13th, 1939. And a wedding date was set tentatively as "after harvest." Elizabeth fondly recalls:

> *Our attraction for each other grew, and in March 1939, Jens Peter Hansen and I were engaged. It was a wonderful summer. On October 15th, Jens and Jake were baptized in the Mennonite Church in Duchess, and Mom was received as a member* (pp. 22, 23).

The living arrangements with Jens Hansen were less than ideal. Jens reserved one bedroom for himself. The Friesen family occupied the other four rooms. Tena described the situation as she remembered it:

> *For the next few years, we lived in extremely congested conditions. We all slept in one large room except the boys, they slept in a small bunk house in our front yard. I envied their privacy and wished for a bunkhouse of my own.*
>
> *Our large room was set up almost like an open hospital ward with bed sheets for curtains and cardboard wardrobes separating us from our parents and giving each bed a feeling of separate rooms. The cardboard wardrobes held our coats and dresses. The rest of our belongings were stored in cardboard boxes under our beds. Every inch of space was used.*

> *Our large dining room table framed by two long benches and two chairs occupied most of the space in our living and dining room combined, which also held a couch and easy chair.*
>
> *We had a very tiny kitchen with a pump inside, a small porch for our boots and winter jackets....*
>
> *Here we had a cistern outside with a pump inside, so we only had to carry the dirty water out. We didn't have any plumbing or electricity.*
>
> *The outdoor biffy was a fair distance from the house, making it shear torture to get to in winter in deep snow in a flimsy dress. Sometimes it was scary to go out there after dark especially alone even when I had a flashlight or lantern....*
>
> *Considering the severe conditions our family had to live in, we all organized extremely well. We did much better with much less than many poor folks did during the lean times... We always managed to do our house cleaning every year. Everybody did their share to make it work, but we were not without huge problems* (pp. 144-147).

To carry on a proper discrete courtship in those restricted conditions was not easy. Helen shares a glimpse of how life was in those quarters:

> *Before Jens and Elizabeth got married, Jens had a cot in his only room. We girls would go in there, sit beside him, sit on his lap, and crawl all over him. What we all talked about I don't know, but we sure entertained him and ourselves. He was always good to us. He was like a father to us youngsters.*
>
> *We girls decided to give Elizabeth a birthday surprise. It must have been 1939. We invited people from our church. We really worked to get ready, raking the big lawn and cleaning the house. The day arrived, and Elizabeth and Jens were sitting in the car with doors open and a cover over top for shade. We girls ran and jumped around, giggling, enjoying our secret. I don't remember who the first people were that arrived, but we surprised the couple. We thought it fun to have them caught courting under this "canopy."*

We girls most always followed them around. They tried to find some privacy, but we eventually found their secret place and sat down with them whether it was in the chicken coup or up in the barn loft, or just in the house.

Jens usually broke his own work horses in the winter. At least one time it was winter, and he hitched his team to a stone-boat, the snow was deep, a good time to keep a horse back a bit. He hitched the unbroken horse with one that was broken and dependable. On this occasion he took Elizabeth along, and of course us youngsters piled on too. We wouldn't miss a chance like that. I wouldn't have known how to act if I would have had to court like that!

Jens's place was four miles straight north of the West Duchess School, so the Friesen children had even further to go. They missed a lot of school and even tried correspondence instead, but that didn't succeed. Going to church was also more difficult. Sometimes Jens would hook up his team and wagon and take Mother Friesen and all the children to church in Duchess.

What little Edward remembers most about those times was the excitement that he felt when the "Watkins man" would visit. This kind peddler always had a small packet of candy or gum for the kids. But Ed always went into hiding when Peter Wiebe showed up, because he had said he was going to take Ed with him!

When they moved, Ed preferred to ride in the wagon rather than Jake's car because the wagon was safe! But he trusted Henry Ramer more than his own brother, for he loved to ride in his new Plymouth to Bible School along with about ten other kids. Despite the severe overload, there were no worries about safety there!

What hurt the children deeply was that the man who bought their farm from under them was one of their own Mennonite "Christians." Helen recalls their feelings:

Melita, Tena, and I were so upset about our having to move, we called after our neighbor when he went past. I don't think he ever heard us, but Mom did, and she scolded us about it. Part of our anger stemmed back to our going to school, I think.

> *This man came to school one day and whispered loudly to the teacher, "How many Friesens are there?" Once again, when Dr. Ens came to school to inoculate the children this man came in and whispered loudly again, "How many Friesens are there?" Some of the pupils snickered.... We were very humiliated.*

The trauma of losing one's farm repeatedly certainly leaves it's scars on the psyche of the one suffering the loss. Tena evaluates the impact of this loss on her dad as well as on the whole family:

> *Prior to 1936 my father worked hard and was still in reasonable health. A farmer always did his own repairs. I did hear of farmers going to the garage for parts when nothing else would do the job and new parts had to be obtained. My father was capable of doing many crafts. He tested ground for water, dug wells and cased them, built cardboard covered sleighs, made drays, buggies, democrats, and he made wheels from scraps. He fixed our shoes, made harnesses from pieces of old ones, and he make kitchen cupboards for the neighbors. My father did not have much of a formal education and he lacked the money to buy nails, string, nuts, bolts, and other materials he needed. Trying to manage a farm with the help of ten small girls and a hard-working wife wasn't enough and we lost our good CPR farm to the collectors.*
>
> *The next five years were sad times. It happened to us, and it happened to others, but a few farmers were lucky. Maybe those who were lucky were better managers, I don't really know.... In 1938 it became obvious how very devastating losing our good farm really was for all of us. The Great Depression destroyed my father at the age of forty. He never started over again. The successive losses of his land made him a very angry man. It was difficult to really understand the change in him. I think he felt he was a failure. Now there was no courage left to start over again, nor did he have the motivation. His health played a part in all of this. I don't know if he lost his farm because of poor management or because of the lack of money, but I believe it was a combination of both. In a way*

> *my father really was a dreamer of dreams, always dreaming out of reality's reach* (p. 144).
>
> *My father became more irritable. It was my mother who constantly tempered his anger. As children we sure didn't understand it. In a way my mother was my father's slave, but she stood by him throughout all of this. Once I asked her why she did it and she said that she believed God put him here to see what people would do with him. It was never easy. She was all he ever had. There never ever was anybody else who really understood him like she did. She knew things about him that were never discussed with the rest of us, and I sure never knew how to cope with such an angry verbally abusive father. I never ever knew what it meant to have a real father. I never ever said "Hi!" to my father in my entire life. I only remember verbal battles and no understanding* (pp. 147, 148).
>
> *We were children of a heavy harsh dust-bowl farmer who had no time for his children's emotional development. I never had a conversation with my father.... He never was a father to me. He never hugged his children, or ever told them he cared about them* (p. 58).
>
> *Seeing my parents lose the farm that I loved had a profound effect on me. I didn't like the man who bought it. He was our Christian neighbor, and in my young mind I figured that a true Christian ought not to take from the poor. I did not tell anybody just how I felt. I always kept things like anger and deep hurt inside.... We survived those bad times because we were made of solid stuff to begin with. Integrity, faith, and a willingness to work hard was in our genes* (p. 145).

Although the matter of laying blame for the disaster that befell the Friesen family is irrelevant today, there was a consensus among the oldest children that their father was not a capable manager. The times were tough, and the world seemed set against him, and his family was large, yet he was given several excellent opportunities to get started farming, and each time he made bad choices and the opportunity passed him by.

In other ways Jacob Friesen was a very talented and clever man. He could do almost anything with his hands. He never had any money or proper tools, or he might have been a very fine carpenter or mechanic. He built rooms onto his houses and barns using scraps. Sometimes he built buildings, renovated houses, and built cupboards for other people. He used to make doll houses and furniture for his girls and carve little toy animals for them.

In later years he always kept his old car and tractor running, often by combining two or more worn out ones. He always was finding jobs in the neighborhood and could do almost anything they wanted done.

He was musically inclined. In later years they had an old pump organ. He would sit and play the old favorites and sing by himself. He could play a guitar or do a polka with an accordion. But because of his disastrous relationship with his children, his efforts were not appreciated very much.

Outside of the home, Jacob Friesen was a very sociable fellow. He had no problem in meeting new people and striking up a conversation.

One cold day after moving to Duchess, he needed to meet someone, so he went up to the door and knocked. When the stranger opened the door, Jacob stretched out his hand and said, "Hello, I'm Friesen!" The man said, "I'm cold too! Won't you come in?"

He loved to talk with anyone who cared to listen. Often, he would meet a total stranger and invite him in for coffee and sit and visit for a few hours. If the man could speak German that was an extra treat! If he knew some Russian or Ukrainian that was also a special challenge. But most of his visiting was done in English.

Jacob just loved to tell stories and maybe spin a little yarn on the side. But his accent was heavy, and his style of storytelling was very disjointed and difficult to follow, so usually the listener was less enthusiastic than the teller and would endure more or less patiently until the tale was over and then excuse himself.

Sometimes when he was in the dining room swapping stories with a friend, his wife would be in the kitchen working and listening. Every now and then, she would whisper to her children, "That's not true; it wasn't that way at all!" So obviously she had her own version of the story, and in the minds of her children their father's credibility suffered a low rating. In fact, they hardly cared to listen to any of his stories and remember very little.

We grandchildren also cared little for his stories, so a large legacy of oral history, with some sleight embellishments granted, was lost to the family when he made his final move to the "city that has foundations."

A Unilateral Declaration of Independence

Fifteen-year-old Jake was working for a farmer floating land for a dollar a day. It was November and getting mighty cold. He had no winter clothes; in fact, his summer clothes were just rags. He would put cardboard in his shoes twice a day because there were holes in the soles. Yet he had no control over his wages, and his dad had other priorities for their use. Jake wanted to respect and honor his father, but he was desperate for some warmer work clothes. He felt over worked, abused, exploited, oppressed, and under-appreciated by his father.

Finally, he went to the local R.C.M.P. officer, and asked him how he could legally get control over his wages and still honor his parents.

The police officer informed him, that, if he would run away to a place his parents couldn't find him, and stay there and work for four months, and support himself and save his money, and then bring some home to help the family, he would be honoring his father and would be considered by the law to be independent.

So that is what Jake did. In 1938, though he was just sixteen, he ran off to Gliechen and found a job, and established his independence. Later, he went to Sundre and worked for a year and a half in farming and logging.

Besides his necessities, he would spend no more than five cents each week for a treat like a chocolate bar or a soda for himself. He saved the rest and brought it all home, but not in cash. He would bring it in clothing and food for the whole family. That way he honored his father, everybody benefited, and he kept control over his earnings.

Later his younger sisters, Neta, Hedy, Helen, and Tena did the same. When they reached fifteen years of age, they quit school and went to work. There were usually jobs for girls in the community. There were potatoes to pick, fields to stook or other harvesting chores in the fall. There were always expectant mothers who needed household help, or a girl to help with the farm chores throughout the year. There was even greater need for household help during spring and summer on the farm.

Neta worked for Jens and Elizabeth. Hedy worked for Sam Martin's for several years. Tena worked for several neighbors. Helen worked the summer of 1943 for Jens and Elizabeth, the summer of 1944 for Levoy Roth's, then after finishing grade nine, she quit school and worked for Levoy's again for a few months and then for Clarence Ramer's for a few months.

For doing housework, a girl would be paid from twenty-five to seventy-five cents a day plus room and board. From their earnings they all saved carefully and helped their family to survive.

A few years later Jake bought his first car; the first car in the Friesen family. Tena was very impressed:

> *Jake gave me my first ever car ride in a black Model T Ford coup with a small lid on its trunk.... This car had a seat for two and couldn't move faster than a mule. It sputtered and popped as he pumped gas and manipulated the choke. There were two speeds of travel; full blast and stand still.*
>
> *We spent most of our day trying to keep the tires inflated.... We patched a lot of holes on the inner tubes using the stuff he carried along in his do-it-yourself kit. There were a lot of round and oblong red rubber patches on those inner tubes by the time we got back from that four-mile trip, but I loved every moment of it. It was a very exciting way for me to spend a nice warm summer Sunday* (p. 25).

World War II and the End of the Depression

The economic conditions were improving slowly and very slightly in 1938 and 1939. Then on September 9th, 1939, Canada declared war on Nazi Germany.

Jens Hansen & brother-in-law to be, Jake Friesen, 1939

Suddenly there were jobs for everybody, and markets opened for the products of their labor. Hundreds of thousands of the finest of Canada's young men were needed for the huge army that was being raised and trained. Factories needed to be built and equipped to produce the war materials that the armed forces would need to succeed in their work. Those factories needed millions of employees to keep them producing at full capacity. And everybody would need food, lots of good nourishing food, so that they could be in top physical condition and give their best for the war effort.

War mania gripped the nation, the hardships of the "dirty thirties" were put behind, and all united together to help Britain in its lonely desperate struggle to defeat tyranny in Europe.

One really wonders that the government had no money to stimulate the economy at home to help its own people during the long depression years, but suddenly there was plenty of money to wage a most terrible war of destruction over in Europe.

The upside of this awful development was that the Great Depression was over! But it would take years for the wounds to heal, and the scars would remain for the rest of the lives of many of the victims. It would take years for the poorest to get back on their feet, and some of them never would. Jacob Friesen was one of those.

He was burned out, and never really tried to get started again. He worked at odd jobs occasionally, and even rented land and farmed a bit, but he was never successful and remained poor until he retired on the Canadian Federal Government's old age pension. His older children took over the responsibility of supporting their mother and the younger members of the family.

Justina and Jacob Friesen in 1939

The Friesen Family in 1930: Back Row, l. to r. Tena, Elizabeth, Jake, Neta, Justina holding baby Martha, Hedy, and Helen. Front row: l. to r. Annie, Melita, Jacob holding Edward, Anita, and Susan

8

Starting a New Generation

Rebekah also looked up and saw Isaac. She got down from her camel and asked the servant, "Who is that man in the field coming to meet us?" "He is my master", the servant answered. So, she took her veil and covered herself.... Isaac brought her into the tent of his mother Sarah, and he married Rebekah. So, she became his wife, and he loved her; and Isaac was comforted after his mother's death. – Genesis 24:64-67 NIV.

The wedding date had been set for "after harvest." In 1939 the harvest time came with bad weather, so it went slow. The eager couple's anxiety level went up another notch with each passing cold wet useless day in October. There must be a harvest and grain must be sold before there could possibly be a wedding. It wasn't just their crop that needed to be threshed, they had to meet their obligations to their neighbors as well who shared the threshing work.

Finally, the bad weather broke, and a nice late "Indian Summer" set in, and the threshing went ahead full steam! As soon as it was completed, they set a date. There wasn't much time left for a "fall" wedding. It needed the services of a pastor, and Clarence Ramer was heading for Tofield to start Winter Bible School on the Sunday afternoon of November 26th. It would suit to have the marriage ceremony that morning. So, it was agreed.

The remaining days were packed with the preparations that inevitably accompany even the simplest wedding. The grain had to be sold. Jens took the Greyhound Bus to Calgary to buy the necessary black suit and new shoes. Elizabeth found a suitable white dress with the lavish price tag of three dollars and matching white shoes for a pricey one dollar and ninety-eight cents.

Jens had taken the step of being baptized by Bishop J.B. Stauffer on October 15th, so now he was a bonafide "Mennonite", and "Hansen" had become a "Mennonite name" and no further obstacles remained for this Dane to marry this Dutch German-Russian-Canadian-Mennonite girl.

The couple made a trip to Moore's Furniture Store in Brooks and bought a bed and a drop-leaf table. They returned along with the furniture delivery truck, bringing along a marriage permit for Mother Friesen to sign. They made it a point to not ask her father to sign it. With the permit signed, they returned to Brooks with the delivery man, finished the legal business, and returned home by bus, with the desired marriage license.

The big day finally came. The wedding was to be a part of the Sunday morning service at the Duchess Mennonite Church. There would be Sunday school first and then the wedding. Bennet Torkelson and Neta Friesen were to be groomsman and bridesmaid. Since Jens didn't have a car at the time, Corny and Lois Siemens were to bring the couple to the service after Sunday school. Corny recalls how it went:

> *Not having a watch, we depended on an old clock on the wall. Not knowing its habits...we began to wonder about the seemingly long morning. Then they told us that the clock had a habit of playing tricks. The hand would go up part way and then drop. Of course, see what it did to our time!*
>
> *We finally decided we better go, and we took our time, after all we had the bride and the groom!*
>
> *Half ways to town, here comes a car sure raising the dust! It was Fred Martin coming to see what had happened. They almost ran out of songs! Well, we got them there! And after forty years it seems like a good deed done!* (Corny Siemens, reminiscing in a speech on Jens and Elizabeth's fortieth wedding anniversary).

The happy couple were late for their own wedding, but the congregation was patient.

They walked up the aisle together unaccompanied and sat on the front bench. Clarence Ramer preached a real wedding sermon for a whole hour. He based his sermon on the story of Abraham finding a wife for his son Isaac: "He that findeth a wife findeth a good thing." (Pr. 18:22). His challenge was: "In all thy ways acknowledge him and he shall direct thy paths."

At length he concluded his edifying exposition with the invitation: "And now, if you are still of the same mind...." Did he really suppose that his words might have changed their minds? Then Henry B. Ramer led them through the marriage vows and pronounced them "man and wife."

There was a surprise wedding reception at their home in the afternoon. Members of the congregation came and brought food and gifts. Although it was late November, the weather was so sunny and warm that people were comfortable to come without coats. They spent the afternoon singing and visiting.

For their honeymoon night, the newlyweds caught the bus to Brooks and found a hotel there. They returned the next day. There simply wasn't money for a more romantic and adventurous trip.

Mr. & Mrs. Jens & Elizabeth Hansen on their wedding day, November 26, 1939, at their home

Starting a New Life Together

After the wedding was over the newlyweds had forty dollars left to see them through seeding time the following spring. Of course, they milked five or six cows and sold cream which helped them survive. They got their winter fuel from the coulee free of charge. When there wasn't any cash, they often resorted to barter.

Since Friesens were still living in the same house, they also shared the yard with Jens and Elizabeth. Tena or Helen usually rode out on the lease land, which was open prairie stretching away to the skyline north and east of the farm, to bring the cows home in the evening. They would help their mother milk them sometimes.

In the winter, the cows were milked in a straw shed, and in the summer, they were milked standing untied in the yard. They would help draw water from the well with a bucket and a rope. In winter it would get icy around the edge of the well from the water spilling and freezing. It was treacherous, especially for the little children. It must have kept one of God's special angels busy. Not one of them fell in!

Helen was an eleven-year-old girl at that time. She made a contract to help the newlyweds. She would fetch the cows and help milk them and do other errands and chores. Elizabeth would record each day she helped and write a credit of five cents. When they added up to thirty-five cents, Helen felt rich.

One day the neighbor's bull got in with their cows. Helen was on their black horse, trying to chase the cows out to the field, but she became frightened of the way the bull looked at her.

So, Tena said, "Let me do it", and she got on the horse. She managed to get the cows out of the gate, but then the bull turned on her. He put his mighty head under the horse and lifted the horse and rider up and dropped them on the fence. They just missed a fence post, so no one was hurt.

Helen ran to tell the neighbor lady about their bull, and all the neighbor said was, "I bet you were scared!"

The most important gain they got that year was the little baby Peter Jens Hansen who was born on September 13, 1940, at the hospital in Rosemary. His mother dug potatoes the day before he was born. He added much joy and congestion in the little house. His grandmother, Justina insisted that the couple take a second room of the shared house. So, his presence was felt by all. Four months later January 30, 1941, Esther Ruth Friesen was born. The walls of the house bulged a few more inches!

When Justina first came to Canada, she did not learn English. But when Elizabeth married a Dane, she realized that she would never be able to understand or talk to her grandchildren unless she learned English. So, she took time out of her busy life to teach herself English. She succeeded very well. She spoke with a heavy accent but was fluent.

That year the crops were good, and the prices were better, so in 1941 Jens bought his first tractor, an old Fordson Major, for $200.

Helen tells of playing in the straw stacks and digging into the straw loaded on the rack.

> *One time Jens had unloaded the rack and there was a pile of straw laying behind the rack. Those days the pigs were free to roam at will and on this occasion, they found the straw pile. Melita and I decided we would climb up the end of the rack and jump down into the straw pile. We were on the rack, and I noticed the straw pile moved a bit. "Ah, yeah, the pigs are under it!", I thought, "This is going to be fun! I'll let Melita jump first!" She jumped and I don't know who was surprised the most, her or the pigs! There were "Ouph!" "Ouph!"s from the pigs as they scattered in every direction. We tried to figure out how to get the pigs under the straw pile again so we could have some more fun. We even went away for a while, but the pigs did not return, they had had enough!*

Elizabeth was impressed with how gentle Jens was with his animals. She wrote:

> *Jens always talked to his animals, almost like they were people. They seemed to understand. One time his old cow was standing in front of a two-wire fence, placidly chewing her cud, when he came along. He lifted one wire and put his foot on the other and talked soothingly, "So you want to get through old girl. Come on, Koh, Koh, come on!" and she walked leisurely through.*

We had a big gangly horse we called Albert. His ears would prick up at his master's voice. One night we had to shorten his suffering with a gun. He'd been sick and couldn't get better. Jens walked up to him, stroked him, and told him it was "too bad, old boy." The horse seemed to understand and whinnied back. (Elizabeth Hansen, in "Jens P. Hansen" an article she wrote for *Duchess and District Memories*, p. 234).

A Second Son is Born

On October 26, of 1941, Elizabeth awoke early in the morning with the discomfort of labor pains. She promptly informed her husband, who shook off his drowsy sleep and went over to awaken his neighbor, Carl Liebert, and to beg him to assist with his car, since it would be very slow, uncomfortable, and cold for the lady in labor to ride the seven miles of bumpy frozen rutted roads to the hospital with the horses and wagon in the chilly darkness of a wintry dawn. Mercifully, Carl Liebert was agreeable and quickly dressed and went out and cranked his fine jalopy until it sputtered to life, then he drove over and picked up the patient and rushed her to the Rosemary Hospital!

The nurses were just waking up and getting themselves ready for the day's duties when the Liebert "ambulance" came chuffing to a halt at the entrance. They quickly brought the patient inside and immediately prepared her for the ordeal. A part of the preparation involved the patient sitting on the toilet. What followed the patient can best describe in her own words:

The nurse accompanying me to the "can" was watching me and at the same time combing her long hair. Sitting there on the "can" I thought I was finished and proceeded to get up to go back to the bed, but the nurse stopped me, and I sat back down again. Next thing I was headed for the floor. She caught me and the other nurses came running and carried me to the case room and the doctor came running. They put me under and the next thing I knew we had a baby son. It was Sunday morning, 7:00 a.m. From the time we arrived at the hospital to the birth had taken about half an hour. He was a big nine pounds and twelve ounces boy. He had come fast and hard.

> *The nurses wheeled me into the room and put me to bed. His dad came. I was in a strange state - not here, not there. It was a very strange feeling, like hanging in space, not here, not there. I think I was in shock. It was that way for a bit and then I could cry and came back to earth again. I felt so bad because everybody would think I cried because it wasn't a girl but that was not the case. They of course couldn't see these other goings on.*

Elizabeth wanted to name the baby "Paul", but Jens wanted to name him after his favorite brother, Karl who had died at age twenty-two of tuberculosis. For some reason, the man's argument held more sway, so the boy became known as "Carl Edward Hansen."

9

Settling into Community

Abraham planted a tamarisk tree in Beersheba, and there he called upon the name of the Lord, the Eternal God. And Abraham stayed in the land of the Philistines for a long time. – Genesis 21:33, 34 NIV.

Now the house was ready to start popping nails! Since Grandmother Friesen was also still giving birth, there was a serious population explosion. Esther was born on January 30, 1941. Now Carl was person number eighteen in that little five-room house. Something had to be done.

To dissipate the looming environmental crisis, Jake contributed one hundred dollars, Neta fifty dollars, and the Duchess Church kicked in fifty dollars, and they bought a good four-roomed CPR house to be moved. Clarence Ramer gave an acre of rent-free land on the corner of his property, and someone brought a caterpillar and moved the house onto the land.

Jacob enclosed the long narrow porch, creating two more small rooms. And Justina scrubbed and cleaned that house and scrapped layers of paint off the living room walls, then painted and polished it until it met her high standard of fitness for human habitation. Nobody asked about lead in the paint in those days!

Thus, by the end of December 1941, the Friesen family vacated the Hansen house, and once more moved their precious belongings, by horse and wagon, to a new home. Thanks to the loyalty of the grown children, their mother would never have to live in other people's houses again.

Jens and Elizabeth in their family "sedan" visiting the Friesen home

Continued prosperity allowed the Hansen family to add to their asset list a new McCormick cream separator, a used sewing machine, a better heater, and a used Model A Ford car in 1942.

In February of 1943, Neta started to work for Jens and Elizabeth. Then on March 25, 1943, another son, Paul Hans Hansen, was born in the Rosemary Hospital. David James Friesen was born in the hospital at Bassano on September 14, 1943. His arrival completed the "Friesen Fourteen", eleven daughters and three sons.

Hansens Move to Clancy

Jens sold his first farm in West Duchess and bought another one about seven miles south of Duchess from the E.I.D. in the Clancy District. It was a half section of good land for which he paid $2500. It was located one-mile due west of the Clancy School. A few weeks after Paul's birth, Jens and Elizabeth moved, with all their belongings, to this new farm in April 1943.

A Conscientious Objector to War

While "war fever" was running very high in the community, Mennonites could not, in good conscience, become active participants in the national effort. Having accepted the logical principle that "No one can serve two masters!" and having already pledged their supreme allegiance to Jesus Christ as their only Lord, to entertain the demand of Fatherland for an equal allegiance was impossible.

As they understood it, Jesus had called them to a life of radical love that was all inclusive, large enough to include the wellbeing of even one's most bitter enemy. Such love sometimes demanded unsolicited and unjust suffering at the very hands of the beloved "enemy." It demanded a stance of non-resistance, or at best, non-violent resistance to evil. Jesus had called them to a higher purpose, a positive life of constructive service in peace-making, reconciliation, development, and meeting human need.

They recognized that Jesus Christ, heading up a "kingdom" that is "not of this world", a kingdom that transcends national boundaries and patriotic sentiments, is not partisan to the petty nationalistic and patriotic divisions of humankind. Hating or killing were strictly forbidden. There was no room for a second equal allegiance to their nation or their government, especially when it demanded their participation in acts of mass destruction and the taking of fellow human life.

The Canadian Government was gracious to young men who held such radical convictions, even in times of war, and made allowances.

In February 1943, Jake Friesen was called to present himself for service to his country. He had registered with the Selective Service beforehand and claimed conscientious objector (CO) status. His case was approved, and he was granted CO status and was given "Agricultural Leave."

This meant that he would have to work on a farm for sixty dollars per month plus room and board. Of this amount he would get to keep twenty-five dollars for pocket money and give thirty-five dollars to the Red Cross. Those who went to camps in the forests got only fifteen dollars per month. Jake served this way for exactly four years.

For three years, he served on Clarence Ramer's farm, and, in 1946, he did agricultural service on the farm of his brother-in-law, Jens Hansen. While working for his brother-in-law, he made a special deal that he would be allowed to rent Jens's quarter section of dry land, if he would build a fill on it and level it, preparing it for irrigation. This he did.

While serving this way, Jake saved every penny he got. With those twenty-five dollars he was allowed to keep each month; he was able to help his parents pay off their immigration debt.

Up to this time, his family and many others had not paid their loans to the CPR. The Mennonite Immigration Board had guaranteed the loans of the immigrants. That was more than twenty years earlier, but because of hardships in getting settled and the disastrous Depression, many had not yet cleared their obligations.

Now times were a bit better, and the Immigration Board set a deadline to clear all debts in 1946. CPR agreed to reduce the interest rate from 6% to 3%, and to cancel all interest since 1934. Jens paid seventy-five dollars for Elizabeth, Neta paid seventy-five dollars for herself, Jacob had paid fifty dollars earlier, and now Jake paid the remainder for his father and mother and seventy-five dollars for himself.

Going to Church

> *Since we have a great priest over the house of God, let us draw near to God with a sincere heart in full assurance of faith.... Let us hold unswervingly to the hope we profess, for he who promised is faithful. And let us consider how we may spur one another on toward love and good deeds. Let us not give up meeting together, as some are in the habit of doing, but let us encourage one another.* – Hebrews 10: 21-25 NIV.

Going to church in those days required a certain amount of commitment. It often involved traveling by horse and wagon or by sleigh if there was snow in winter. Even if they had cars, they would face the hazards of the dirt roads: snow and ice and cold drafts in the winter, and muddy rutted tracks or clouds of dust percolating in through the cracks, in the summer.

Mennonites were faithful in attending church, even though it sometimes required a major struggle to get there. Could we, their descendants, take our loyalty to our Creator and Sustainer, and our participation in the community of God's people to the same level today? Certainly, with our affluent lifestyle with reliable and comfortable vehicles, good roads, and fine worship centers, the excusable obstacles have been minimized.

The Mennonite Church building at Duchess was a plain white wooden structure with grey shingled roof and black trim. It was rectangular in layout with front steps and main entry with cloak rooms centered at one end, a central aisle with pews and rectangular windows along both sides, and a special windowed alcove at the back that contained the pulpit on a raised platform. Three special benches facing each other on each side of the pulpit constituted the "amen corner" or "Deacon's bench" which were usually occupied by the elderly brothers and sisters on their respective sides. It had a high peaked roof which afforded a high ceiling inside.

In line with Anabaptist rejection of "temples," "sacramentalism," and "sacerdotal hierarchy," this "meeting house" was functional, and plain, inside and outside, without embellishments of images, crosses, stained-glass windows, or steeple. The essence of the "church" was, and would always be, the "people of God," not buildings nor organizations. In the church of Jesus Christ, there are no sacred places, no sacred offices, no sacred vestments, no sacred objects, nor sacred words, only sacred people. Whether gathered or scattered, where the people of God are, there one finds the true visible "church."

The men and their sons sat on the right side in the meeting room, and the mothers sat on the left, with their daughters and the babies. The meetinghouse was usually full, and one could smell the sweat of the men, as the temperature rose, and the oxygen supply was depleted. Deodorant was not yet a common commodity in those days. If somebody opened the window too wide, somebody else was sure to feel the draft and have it closed.

Children had to sit quietly in church. Nonsense was not tolerated during the service. If their parents did not control them, the preacher would call them to order from the pulpit. There would certainly follow another session at home if that ever occurred! But it was tiresome at times. The sermons were long, and there was little in them that could hold a child's attention.

Many of the men wore regulation "plain suits", of somber colors without lapels that had short upright military-style collars similar to those worn by Catholic priests. Of those that didn't wear the "plain suit", none wore neckties. No jewelry was allowed, and one could be refused communion for wearing even a wedding band.

Many of the women wore plain colored regulation dresses that had capes. Many a sermon exhorted the women on the virtues of wearing the "cape dress," yet a lot of the women were not convinced.

The women would not even think of cutting their hair or of wearing a hat. While inside, they wore the traditional Mennonite style "prayer veiling" on their heads. It was a neat little white starched cap made of netting material that generally fit the contours of the head often enclosing the hair that was done up in a "bun" at the back of the head. Sometimes this veil was tied under the chin with thin ribbons or "covering strings." Some women wore them with the strings hanging loose down their backs. Some didn't have strings at all. Outside they wore kerchiefs, scarves, or bonnets to cover their heads.

Sunday morning activities at the church would start with a devotional exercise including songs, Bible reading, prayer, and comments on the lesson, which of course bypassed the small minds. Then adults and children alike went to their Sunday school classes.

Mary Ramer, the wife of Henry, the elderly preacher, was a favorite Sunday school teacher with the small children.

After Sunday school, the children would reassemble with their parents in the auditorium, carrying their "Words of Cheer" or "Beams of Light", whichever take-home paper they were qualified to receive. The Sunday school superintendent would make some appropriate comments and allow some minutes for discussion.

Although we Mennonites prided ourselves in being a "non-liturgical church," we still held to a very predictable program that held very little deviation from the pattern set by our ancestors.

After the Sunday school was dismissed, there would be a few minutes of noisy readjustment as everybody left their classes and re-assembled for the worship service.

The preacher and the deacon would take their places on the platform behind the pulpit. The chorister, usually Joe Martin, would lead two songs. All songs were sung a cappella, as musical instruments were not allowed.

The deacon, Marlin Brubaker, would stand up behind the pulpit, read a passage of scripture, make a few comments, and ask all to kneel while he led in prayer. Everyone would turn around and kneel into their benches. Then the deacon knelt beside the pulpit and, with face upturned, and sometimes hands raised, prayed a prayer of worship and supplication that left no doubt in young minds that here was a man who really knew God.

The deacon's prayer was usually long enough for young boys to search for deposits of used gum under the benches, examine other people's shoes, and even pull a leg or two if the owner was judged young enough to appreciate the humor. If the discovery of someone's abandoned gum was fruitful, we would try teasing the dry amorphous mass loose from its sticky perch. I wouldn't use it. For me there was a certain exhilaration in the success of discovery and recouping it. But my gum-deprived younger brother discovered that it was recyclable!

When the deacon's prayer finally came to an end, the offering was taken, announcements made, and another song sung.

Then the preacher would take his place behind the pulpit while the deacon retired to his seat on the front bench. The preacher often spoke for three quarters of an hour, although sometimes his inspiration stretched his extemporaneous sermon to a whole hour.

There would then be a "closing song" of response by the congregation, and the preacher would lead in a benedictory prayer and dismiss the people.

Following dismissal, however, most of the people didn't rush off home. They would loiter around visiting one another. This fellowship was an important part of what it meant to be a "people of God," a "community of the committed," the essence of what it means to be "church."

There were three preachers in the Duchess congregation: Henry B. Ramer, an older pioneer and founding father of the congregation, Clarence J. Ramer, his son and current bishop, and Paul Martin, a youth recently ordained "by lot" at eighteen years of age.

All these ministers were farmers who worked hard to support themselves and their families, and never received any financial remuneration for the services they rendered to the church and the community. They were sons of the community, were called to the ministry by lot, and were ordained to serve God and his church for life.

They never expected to be transferred or to move to another church.

They were usually not trained, although Clarence had four years of Bible College training and was a life-long student of Bible, history, and current affairs. His sermons were packed with information and were impressive.

When it seemed right to choose a new church leader, either to help an aging one, or to replace one that passed on or moved away, the "lot" was used to discern whom God was calling to be his minister.

First the decision to ordain a man was announced in advance, and all were called to a time of heart-searching urgent prayer, That God just might prefer they ordain a woman, was never a consideration. Then a date and time was set, usually after a Sunday morning service, to hear the counsel of the church.

At that time, each member, one by one, passed before the bishop and ministers and gave the name of the person from among them, that he or she felt was "called" to be their new minister. Sometimes only one name was given. In such cases it became obvious that God had chosen and equipped that person to bear the responsibility to shepherd the "flock." An ordination would follow shortly. But usually, several names would be given.

If so, in the next few weeks, the bishop and the ministers would visit each of the named persons, check up on their spiritual lives and ask them whether they felt in their spirits any sense of the call of God in their lives to this level of service. If anyone responded in the affirmative, they were asked if they would be willing to test this sense of call by submitting it to the Lord to be confirmed by lot.

Then a special Sunday for ordination was set, and all the members were urged to be in deep prayer for God to reveal his will. On that day, all those who met the requirements and were willing to test their sense of call, were announced to the congregation and were asked to leave the room.

Then the leaders chose as many hymn books as there were candidates, placed a piece of paper in one of them on which were written the words: "The lot is cast into the lap, but it's every decision is from the Lord" (Pr. 16:33 NIV). The paper was not visible when the book was closed. All the books were arranged in a row on a table at the front. Sometimes an extra book was added, just in case the Lord had other plans.

When the candidates were all invited in, each was asked to take one of the books. The bishop in charge then examined each one's book. The one in who's book the paper was found was usually ordained that same afternoon, and he was often expected to preach his first sermon immediately after.

In a letter, Martha remembers the happy day she fixed her choice in a church service:

> *The Goshen College Quartet was going to be singing in our church this Friday evening in August 1947. That morning I was very sick and fell asleep in the afternoon. When I awoke, I was well again and had a terrible fear come over me that it was the next day and I had missed the program. Anita helped me to realize it was still Friday.*

> *I had a new yellow dress with lace and little red roses on the front which I proudly wore. I was nine years old. Paul Erb preached about the "ninety and nine," the quartet sang the song, and on invitation in the very front row in church, I promptly stood up straight and tall and proud. Neta shook my hand afterwards. I think she was proud too, but I never understood that then. I was baptized on my tenth birthday which was Thanksgiving Sunday, October 12.*

Their mother and all the Friesen family joined the Duchess Mennonite Church except for Jacob. He had been baptized by the Mennonite Brethren in Sedalia, and that would have to do. He was a bit negative and critical and aloof of the Duchess Mennonites who were of Pennsylvania-Swiss origins, though he usually attended the services with his family.

At home on Sunday afternoons, after he acquired a radio in the mid-fifties, he usually listened to Billy Graham and his "Hour of Decision" program.

10

Surviving Good Times

The Lord will send a blessing on your barns and on everything you put your hand to. The Lord your God will bless you in the land he is giving you. The Lord will establish you as His holy people, as He promised you on oath, if you keep the commands of the Lord your God and walk in his ways. – Deuteronomy 28:8-9 NIV

The one acre, on which the Friesen family's house stood, was really unsatisfactory. Situated on the edge of an alkali slough, the soil was sticky clay when wet and very hard and unworkable when dry. It was loaded with solenitzic salts and would grow little besides foxtail. Justina Friesen depended on a prolific garden to feed her prolific progeny. She was totally defeated by the impossible soil conditions prevailing there.

The family became aware of an opportunity to solve that problem. A ten-acre plot of land with a barn and a two-room house on it came up for sale. It was just north of the railroad tracks, half of a mile west of Duchess. There was a cistern just outside the house connected with a hand pump and sink inside. No more dipping water out of a well in the winter. They would only have to carry out the wastewater. The soil was good for gardening. It could be purchased for $1,200.

Once again, the children prayed and then pitched together, especially Tena, Helen, and Hedy, and from their meager earnings contributed their money and, with help from some generous men from the church, they bought it. Wages in those days were about seventy-five cents a day for unskilled labor.

On a cold wintry November day in 1947, the four-roomed CPR house was jacked up and moving skids were placed underneath, and a caterpillar pulled it to the new farm about a mile away. Esther and David were so afraid that the roof would fall on their heads.

This was the first time the Friesen family moved without having to pack a single dish into a single box. Everything remained on the shelves or in the cupboards.

At the end of its brief journey, the house was set down on the ground beside the two-roomed shack about three feet apart from it. Jacob Friesen then cut out and built a large archway joining the two. Now the family had two additional large rooms to serve as kitchen and dining room. The former kitchen-dining-living room could now be just a living room. And a cellar hole underneath provided a good place to store vegetables.

The Friesen CPR house being moved from the Ramer corner to the new acreage across the tracks

Neta Broadfoot's sketch illustrating the conjoining of the two houses into one

The two-roomed house had the luxury of linoleum on its floors; no slivers to watch out for on bare feet. Tena led the family in organizing the wallpapering of the new house. Gradually new furniture was added to the living room. A gas iron was found to replace the old sad irons. Hedy bought a gas-powered washing machine for $125 to replace the old hand-powered wooden one. The children would not have far to walk to school. Things were getting better and better at the Friesen house.

This little farm "across the tracks" would be home for the remaining years until the last of the children finished school and departed to start lives on their own. Justina grew the best gardens on the fertile irrigated soil. She often earned a little spending money by selling surplus vegetables. There was pasture for a couple of cows that supplied them with milk for the family and some cream which Justina sold. Of course, there were chickens and eggs too. She also earned a little cash by doing laundry for road crews, or men from work camps nearby, or by selling handwork such as crocheted things which she made herself.

Susan remembers the garden and its products:

> *A garden sprinkled with the splendor of different colors was mother's special project and delight. Often, one would see her on the Sabbath day, as she strolled through her garden. Then she would return to the house with a dainty sprig in her hand, or a spectacular bouquet, to adorn the evening meal. Beauty was discovered in a new seed, planted in the soil, to die, bear fruit and provide for her family throughout the severe winter months.*
>
> *When the winter winds howled and the blizzards swept across the open prairie, mother's dirt cellar was well stocked. One bin was filled high with potatoes, another with carrots. Cabbage and other storable vegetables filled other bins. Canned fruit and vegetables in jars filled the wooden shelves. Jams and jellies all told of tedious hours spent in preparation for the long winter.*
>
> *Especially pretty to me was the preserved jelly which my mother made from the thorny buffalo berry. The task of patiently picking this berry from the thorny branches was*

> *rewarded by the sparkling, amber-yellow colored exquisite sour tasting product* (excerpted from an unpublished manuscript by Susan Friesen).

An old saying goes like: "A man works from dawn to setting of the sun; but a woman's work is never done!" That certainly was true in the life of Justina, the mother of fourteen. Of course, she taught her children to help with some of the work: cooking meals, packing lunches, baking bread every few days, stoking fires, carrying out ashes, sewing clothes, washing clothes, ironing clothes, patching clothes, cleaning house, milking cows, cooling the cream by setting it in cool water (they had no fridge), besides gardening and irrigating the farm in the warm season, and making quilts and comforters, knitting sweaters or mittens, and crocheting doilies in the winter season.

In the spring potato growers would drop off crates of potatoes to be cut into pieces for planting. She and her children would sit for days cutting potatoes. She got paid by piecework for this service.

Seldom did she sit with her hands idle. If she did in the evenings, after the work of the day was done, it would be to read her Bible and meditate, refreshing her spirit. She did also read church papers, the "*Farm and Ranch Review*", and "*The Western Producer*", the only intellectual stimulation the family could afford. They had no T.V. and got a radio only in the mid 1950's. Yet despite such poverty, they were quite knowledgeable people.

Sometimes, at the end of a busy day, Justina would take time out for reflection. Susan reminisces of a typical quiet summer evening as darkness began to set in around the fading glow of the western sky:

> *Hinges screeched as Mother slowly pushed open the swinging garden gate. She paused quietly, a feminine and frail figure. Dressed in an ankle length, brightly patterned frock with mid sleeves, she loosened her white cotton kerchief from her head. It fell to her small shoulders. Her long brown hair was sprinkled with silver gray. She had it styled in a round, braided knob on her head. Stray wisps of hair swirled about her cheeks. Brown eyes clearly mirrored goodness and joy. They sparkled with the zest for living. Slender lips parted in a soft smile as she exulted*

in the beauty of creation, the sight and sounds of a gorgeous evening.

Suddenly, she uttered, "Mein Gott! Mein Gott!" How she still missed them! Loneliness engulfed mother's soul as she stood by the garden gate. Her thoughts had taken wing to her childhood days - to her family, her home and her country, the great land of Russia. How long! How long! Eternally long! She had parted from her loved ones - launched out into a new unknown land, a new unknown life. Courageously she had embraced the cares and challenges which life had thrust upon her through the years. But always, she clung to the hope of re-uniting, of meeting once again her loved ones so far - an ocean and a continent away.

A shaft of light from her neighbor's house across the creek disturbed her reveries. How late it had become.

The cottage door creaked loudly as mother entered. In the darkness she reached for a match, struck it, and lit the kerosene lamp. Its glass chimney gleamed in the dimness. Always clean and sparkling! Mother carried the lamp into the dining room and adjusted its wick. The lamplight cast shadows across the room.

A rough wooden bench and some chairs were placed around the long table. In one corner of the room was a painted white bookshelf. Its shelves were filled with different sized books, some ancient and others with no covers. Some had ragged edges. Some were new. There were German books, and some were in English.

Beside the bookshelf was a heavy, brown organ with a German hymnal open on the music rack. One pumping pedal was almost broken. Wedding photographs of older children adorned the top of the organ.

Nearby, a cedar chest Jake had made for his mother caught one's attention. Houseplants were on it. The plants were blooming in a myriad of different colors and in various stages of growth.

> *A motto graced the wall. The words "Gott Est Die Liebe" were inscribed on it* ("God is Love").
>
> *Mother reached for "The Calgary Herald." Dad usually brought the paper home from the neighbors. School textbooks were piled high on several wooden chairs. After scanning the newspaper, Mother reached for her Bible.*
>
> *Some time later, exuberant voices broke the stillness and the kitchen door banged vigorously "Mom is still up!", several voices announced in unison. Lively young people dashed in, back from their evening out.*
>
> *Yes, Mom was still up! In the light of an old-fashioned lamp, she appeared tired. She looked up with a smile, a tender glow in her weary countenance. Loath to retire before her youngest, David, was safely home, she had waited up.* (excerpted from an unpublished manuscript by Susan Friesen).

Justina was a peaceable person. She never got involved in controversial issues in the church or community. She minded her own business and expected others to do the same. She set a good example for her children, but never dictated to them what they should do or believe. If they broke some of the Church's rules, like girls cutting their hair, she never condemned them. She allowed them freedom to choose whether they would finish school, the kind of training they wanted, or the kind of career they entered. Overall, she didn't interfere in their courtships or object to their choices of marriage partners although on a few occasions she did see fit to raise some concerned questions.

Esther says:

> *I think Mom could have stepped in when she felt she should or saw the need. I had a Mennonite lady for a teacher in grade six with whom I never got along. She didn't get along with any students and was in the habit of sending pupils home and saying, "and don't ever come back!" Well, the next day they would be back with their parents.*
>
> *One day she told me to go and not come back. My older brother, Ed, and sisters said I shouldn't go back. Mom just kept*

> *quiet and let me stay home for a week. Then parent-teacher conference came up, so she went to see my teacher. She told my teacher, knowing who she professed to be and who I was, we should get along better, and needless to say, I returned to school. Mom never made a fuss, just stated facts* (Esther Visser, in a letter, 1989).

Most of these ten acres was kept for pasture for the cows and the few horses they still used for riding and cultivating the garden. Jacob tried farming again. He rented the "Saum place" east of the road for several years. He acquired an old John Deere "D" and a few pieces of old machinery and tried to farm with them. His efforts earned him something, but it could hardly be described as "successful." Jacob did his own repairs, often combining two or more tractors to keep one running. He also acquired an old car and devoted his talents to keeping it roadworthy.

The family continued to depend quite heavily on the garden for food and the earnings of older children for extras.

Edward remembers the time when a neighbor offered his dad two buckets of eggs free, if he could get them home on horseback without breaking any of them. He succeeded! Two whole buckets of free eggs!

Esther remembers the hot summer day when her dad left his farm work and took her and David to town in his car for ice cream cones and pop at the Duchess Café, which was then owned and operated by two jolly "old" Chinamen. A rare treat! In those days ice cream cones were five cents, and pop was ten cents.

Another time her dad gave her twenty dollars after harvest. It was the biggest money she had ever had to spend. She bought her first reversible pleated skirt of which she was very proud.

David remembers the generosity of his parents in always being willing to share the little they had. In particular, he appreciated the hospitality they showed towards an Indigenous friend who, every spring, walked along the railroad track from the reservation at Gleichen in search of summer work, and who returned in the fall. He would always stop at the Friesen house, where he would be provided with a good supper and a room for the night. It was a disappointment to them all when the visitor no longer made his annual appearances.

Reflections: Meanwhile Back in Russia

Although Jacob and Justina often felt the pangs of homesickness, and missed their families back in Russia terribly, and though they endured a lot of hardships in adjusting to the Canadian scene, especially during the Great Depression, they never regretted the decision they made to migrate out to Canada. And though it was difficult to keep in touch with their families back in Russia, Jacob, and especially, Justina did manage to carry on limited correspondence by letter.

This was particularly tough during the first thirty years of the Stalinist era. Upon their departure back in 1924, the political situation had not yet settled in Russia. Vladimir Ilyich Lenin, head of the recently formed Union of the Soviet Socialist Republics (USSR), died on January 21, 1924. Joseph Stalin was just consolidating his deadly grip on the whole Communist movement when they departed. Under the Stalinist rule, oppression of religious minorities became almost unbearable. By 1929 he closed the door to any emigration of Mennonites or any other dissidents out of the USSR.

This meant that no more of the Friesen nor Warkentin relatives could migrate out. Even letter writing became extremely sensitive. Fear of censorship was the rule of the day. No one knew whether his/her letters were being censored. Many of them were.

They could not write the bad things, and there were few good things to write about. They wrote in code language. The recipients in the west had to "read between the lines," guessing on what the reality behind the statements might be. Correspondents in the free world had to be careful lest what they say might get the recipient into trouble with the secret police. Consequently, while the exchange of correspondence assured each side that the sender was alive, it didn't answer the burning questions of how they were really coping.

After the fall of the USSR in 1989, and the opening of the borders, many of the Russian Mennonites relocated to Germany, and the cousins were able to re-establish contact through personal visits, a lot of information was shared about the suffering they endured in those dark days.

Back when Jacob and Justina were preparing to emigrate, Justina's oldest brother, Aaron Warkentin, was also cleared to go, but his wife was sick and couldn't go. He could not walk out on his sick wife, though he was urged by some to do so. She died later, but by then the Stalinists had closed the doors. Aaron was trapped in Russia.

Years later we learned of the tragedy that followed. His first wife died without children. His second wife produced two living children, Liese and Jacob, and died in birthing twins who also died. His third wife died in giving birth to Johnny in 1937. Aaron's mother, Elisabet, the children's grandmother died in February 1938.

Then in June, Aaron also died at age 47. He was sick at home with kidney stones for a long time. No medical treatment was provided. He could not work and suffered terribly. He was dying in bed when the Communists came with their truck to round up all the German men to take them to work camps (The Soviet Government was preparing for the possibility of another war against Hitler's Germany at that time).

Since he could not walk out, they backed the truck up to the window and were bent on taking Aaron out by force. The neighbors came out en mass and begged for mercy. Here was a dying man without a wife and mother, with a house full of starving children. The Communists relented and he died at home the following week, June 1938.

Justina's other brother, their uncle, Nicholai, took the children. When Nicholai died three years later (Jan. 24, 1943), their aunt, Marie, took the survivors in and raised them for an additional six years.

Then the Communists took the German adults away and left the children to forage for themselves. Little Johnny died in 1945 of starvation, age eight. Liese and Jacob survived and moved to Germany after the fall of the Soviet Union in the early 1990's.

Uncle John

John A. Warkentin, who had emigrated from Russia with his sister, Justina, and her family in 1924, never really settled down to living in one place, nor to pursue a serious career, nor to take on responsibilities other than for himself. For a couple of years, he lived with the Friesen family in their congested and poverty-stricken conditions. Later, he spent most of his winters living around Saskatoon or Borden, Saskatchewan, with old friends.

During the warm season he practically lived in his old car. He was a travelling salesman then, selling newspapers and magazines, or Watkins and Rawleigh products all over southern Saskatchewan and Alberta.

For a few years around 1929 or 1930, John worked for a traveling road show and musical group as a magician and fortune teller. Admission to his show was ten cents. Years later he still had his crystal ball, scarves, posters, black velvet bag, and other paraphernalia which he kept in a locked box. He kept it with him when he was living with the Friesens.

One day when he was out, Jacob and Jake broke into the box to see what it was he kept there that no one was to know about. They saw all these things. John was furious when he discovered this breach of privacy, but it wasn't his home, so what could he do about it?

In later years he found an empty house southeast of Rosemary belonging to David Enns. He got permission to move in. This became his summer home for many years. As he travelled around, if someone would give him a meal or a night's lodging and listen to his stories, he might give him a free subscription to a magazine.

It was said that, at one time, he was engaged to be married to a nice Christian girl, but for reasons known only to himself, he broke off the arrangement and never tried to find another.

John was a thin but heavy-boned man of about five feet and nine inches tall. He was a bit stooped at the shoulders with his head and neck somewhat forward. This appearance was enhanced by a very pronounced thick Hollander's lower jaw that protruded just enough to give him the look of a tough fellow. His large head was very bald with a fringe of grey-brown hair around the sides. His mouth and face lines had the appearance of a perpetual scowl, which could break into an occasional grin that revealed some missing teeth.

He almost always wore a felt hat tilted forward at a cocky angle, whether he was outside or inside. He always wore trousers and long-sleeved shirts of dark grey-charcoal or brownish colors. The trousers were held up with suspenders. His right index fingers were yellowed, and his person reeked of stale smoke.

John turned out to be a rather eccentric and cynical sort of fellow. As Tena says, "It seemed by the way he spoke, he had made up his mind fairly early in life that hell was not somewhere hidden in the bowels of this earth but right here if only people would open their eyes, and that, if there was a heaven, it was reserved for the rich and the lucky."

In later years, he was obsessed with the idea that the police were watching him and harassing him. He thought the Government was against him too. He would write letters to the Prime Minister and to the Queen, as if they knew him. He was a very negative person, and most of the time his complaining didn't make sense to more normal people.

Sometimes John lived like a parasite, mooching off the generosity of his relatives or other compassionate people. He moved in with the Friesens when there was little food and absolutely no room for another person, especially a single man who needed a separate room. He never helped with the work of the farm.

In the summer of 1947, he settled in to live with his niece, Elizabeth, and her family for a few months. He slept in their upstairs guest room. At night he would have the worst nightmares and would scream as one tormented. They sometimes wondered what devils were bothering him. What effect did his life, as a magician with the circus, have on his spirit? Or was it some undiagnosed "post-traumatic stress disorder" resulting from experiences during those troubled times back in Russia?

Baby George was sitting in his highchair pounding on his table. Uncle John said, "He is going to be a preacher!" The boys didn't really like this negative eccentric relative around very much. He wouldn't lift a finger to help Elizabeth around the house, though he ate at her table regularly.

One day she was very busy and asked him to fetch a pail of water, and his reply was, "Give me twenty-five cents and I'll fetch you some water." At that point, she lost all interest in sharing further hospitality with her uncle, and soon after, he was asked to move on.

On one occasion, the Hansen family was visiting in the Friesen home while Uncle John was also living there. Seven-year-old Peter and Esther discovered that John had a bad temper. They began doing things to aggravate him.

Whatever they were doing, they went one step too far and John's safety valve popped. All at once, he came charging out of his room and swung his big fist at Peter with full force. Fortunately, Peter ducked just in time, and John struck the wall with a mighty blow. Peter, and all the other tormentors, didn't give him a second chance. They were afraid of him after that.

11

Spreading Out

I will give you and your descendants the land on which you are lying. Your descendants will be like the dust of the earth, and you will spread out to the west and to the east, to the north and to the south. All peoples on earth will be blessed through you and your offspring. I am with you and will watch over you. – Genesis 28:13-15 NIV.

Hansens Seek Utopia in Ontario

Farming was going better, but Jens was getting restless. Irrigating was hard labor, there were other parts of Canada where rainfall was abundant, and crops flourished without irrigation.

An article appeared in the "Monitor," a Church paper, telling of a church planting mission near Alma, Ontario. It portrayed glorious farming opportunities in the community there and urged Mennonites to move to the area and help the new mission. Jens and Elizabeth's best friends, the Dave and Levoy Roth families, both had moved there in search of a better life in Ontario, so, they decided to sell their farm and follow.

The farm was sold to Malcom Dowling in the fall of 1948, and the family prepared to move. Baby Charles Robert was born in the Brooks hospital on October 18th. Then Jens took the train to Ontario to look for a place to live. After he returned, they had an auction sale in late November and sold everything. They moved to Ontario by train in December 1948.

In Ontario, Jens and Elizabeth bought a farm one mile northeast of Bosworth School between the towns of Drayton and Alma. It had a large cement brick house and a big barn. They bought this farm of one hundred and fifty acres of land with twenty cows, a few calves, some pigs, four horses, and a bit of old horse drawn machinery for a total of $16,000. They had to take out a big loan to make the purchase.

Jens and Elizabeth lived and farmed in Ontario for seven years. They wanted a daughter, so they made an application to the Children's Aid Society to adopt one. Little fourteen-month-old Linda Marie joined the family on February 29, 1952. Her petite body and blue eyes and fine golden-brown curls added a touch of beauty to a rather monotonous-looking family.

They bought an additional 100-acre farm across the road from their original one, bought a good line of up-to-date farm machinery, and rented another 100 acres of pasture for their growing dairy herd. During that time, their five boys grew. Peter completed eighth grade in 1955, and started helping on the farm, and little Charles started grade two.

Hansens Migrate Back to Alberta

Ontario was a good place to live, and Jens and Elizabeth had a good farm and were getting ahead financially. But they were not settled in their minds to stay. Much of the time they were homesick for Alberta and the home and family they left there. Elizabeth didn't like the big cold drafty house. She didn't like the damp cool climate that made her arthritic joints ache. She wasn't happy about the church situation there. And, most of all, she longed to be closer to her family.

Jens didn't like keeping the cows in the damp, sweaty, stinky barn. He longed for the clear dry open skies of the prairies where he could keep the animals outside and feed them on the clean snow, and where he never had to fork their manure.

Then one day in November of 1955, John Santing brought his Dutch father-in-law, Mr. Radstake, to look at the place. They liked it and bought it.

The boys were very unhappy, their dreams were shattered. Ontario was their home. Their friends were there. Their memories were rooted there. They did not want to move. And yet, the decision had been made. The agreement of sale signed. The deed was done. There was no turning back.

Jens bought a nice light blue 1953 Oldsmobile Super 88, a beauty that had a big V-8 engine and automatic transmission and radio. They packed and shipped a few things by rail to Alberta but sold most of their household things to Radstakes. Then there was a round of farewell appointments.

Finally on February 20, 1956, they loaded their suitcases and all eight of themselves into the Oldsmobile and drove away from all that was familiar into a future that was unknown. The boys were disappointed, angry, and bitter. Yet, they tried to be open minded about the possibilities of a bright future in Alberta.

Five days and four nights later they arrived in Duchess at the Friesen house. It was already dark on that Friday evening, and no one noticed the car drive into the yard. Peter went to the door to ask if they could "give a poor guy a bite to eat?" Esther came to the door in answer to his knock. She turned and said to her mother, "Mom, There is a bum out here who wants something to eat!" Grandmother came to see, and said, "Ah Peter!" She knew him immediately, his 215 lb. bulk notwithstanding.

Jens had purchased a farm of 169 acres from Mr. Skrobot for $16,000. It was located on the east side of the main highway between Duchess and Brooks, one mile south of the Clancy School. Later, in the spring they discovered that half of the farmland was ruined with alkaline salts that had oozed up from the subsoil through too many years of over-irrigating. It was useless and could grow nothing.

He had bought the farm in the winter while it was covered with snow and assumed it was good soil. The failure of the land plunged the Hansens into poverty. They had to rent other land to make a living in farming. How they longed for the prosperity they had experienced in earlier times, but it didn't return.

> Peter left the farm and went on his own to work out. The others went to school in Duchess. On November 4, 1956, Freda Joy was born in the Brooks hospital, topping off the family at five boys and two girls.

On November of 1961, after eking a living out of that farm for six years, Jens and Elizabeth sold it to Herman Grossfield, the next-door neighbor, who added it to his operation. The selling price was $18,000.

They in turn bought a half section of land two miles east of Duchess with an old four-roomed CPR house for $10,000. They moved their cattle over to the new farm in the spring of 1962 and seeded the crop. Then they worked on fixing the house during the summer. All this time, the family was still living in the Skrobot farm house. They were able to move into their renovated house after harvest in the fall of 1962.

Carl helped put in the crop on the new farm that spring, worked for John Barg that summer, and then headed east to attend Eastern Mennonite College in Virginia at the end of August 1962. He would spend the next five years there, marrying an American girl, Vera King, in 1964, and having his first child, Cindy, in 1965.

Jake "Steers His Own Ship"

Jake had completed his obligations to the Selective Service of his country and cleared his family's obligations to the CPR in 1946. In 1947 he was finally free to establish his own autonomy, do something for his own future. So, he began courting a special girl from Guernsey, Saskatchewan. Wilma Weber was just the right kind of girl that could add some zip to Jake's here-to-fore difficult and depressing life. So, they planned for a fall wedding.

Jake arranged to rent a farm with a house near Duchess. He thought he had all the arrangements ready and went to Guernsey to prepare for the wedding. Three days before the wedding, he got a phone call informing him that the rental contract was cancelled. What should he do? The couple decided to go ahead with the wedding plans anyway.

On November 16, 1947, Jake and Wilma became "husband and wife." They went back to Alberta and lived with Elizabeth for a week until he could find another farm to rent. But it had only a "bachelor shack" for the newlyweds to call "home."

John Martin gave the newlyweds, as a wedding gift, one acre of land along the highway just north of Duchess. On this land, Jake and Wilma built a sturdy little frame house, measuring twenty-four feet by twenty feet. After living in that "tiny house" or "love nest" for the first year of their married life, they sold it. It had cost them $800.00 to build, and a year later they sold it for $1400.00. They felt rewarded for their labor. The buyer moved it to Brooks.

The Conference leadership approached the young couple with the suggestion that they might consider moving north to Smith to help in a church planting mission there. After selling their house, they moved, with their little son, Ronald, in December of 1949.

Life in the Northern Alberta bush was harsh, and their labor unrewarding. The family lived in a log cabin for most of the sixteen winters they stayed there. Jake cleared land; cut and sold fence posts; tried to farm; worked in the bush or in road construction to supplement his income; hunted and trapped for the same reason; and struggled to keep food on the table for his six children. They ate a lot of bear, elk, moose, deer, and even beaver, and supplemented their diet with wild strawberries, blue berries, saskatoons, and other fruits from the bush.

The church work took a lot of their energies. Sometimes it grew, and then other times it shrunk, as new people would come for a while and then move away to more prosperous communities. Farming was not very good there, and employment opportunities were rather limited. Sometimes Jake and Wilma became very discouraged. They finally moved back to the Duchess community in April 1965. There Jake worked for the E.I.D. as a "ditch rider" for several years.

Neta Serves as a Caregiver to the Needy

Neta went to Ontario where she visited her sister Elizabeth's family and attended the Ontario Mennonite Bible School in January 1950. There she met Jack Broadfoot, a tall handsome bachelor farmer from Watrous, Saskatchewan. She graduated in the spring of 1950 and was the valedictorian. She helped her sister on the farm that summer, then worked at the Braeside Home for the Aged in the winter of 1950-51.

In the next two years, she worked at the Morningside Mission in Toronto, helping with underprivileged children. She worked on a survival budget as a volunteer with several other single women, sometimes not getting enough to eat. She was a very sincere and dedicated Christian.

Sometimes Neta would take a break and go to visit the Hansens. She would always help on the farm when she went, cooking, cleaning, gardening, picking raspberries, and sometimes milking the cows. She would always sing while she worked. She was generally cheerful, talkative, friendly, and always ready to laugh. Elizabeth really appreciated having her sister there as she missed her large family very much. The boys appreciated having her around too because that meant they didn't have to do so much of the housework or garden work.

But sometimes they resented their aunt, especially when she gave so much advice to their mom, on how they should be raised.

The boys hated to wear bib overalls. After a lengthy debate, they finally won their mother over to allow them to wear blue jeans or slacks without suspenders.

Then Neta came to visit and lamented the absence of the overalls and suspenders. The boys were alarmed that their mother might be influenced to retract their newly won freedom. But when they complained about Neta, Elizabeth just said, "I really hope that she has a bunch of boys of her own someday!"

In later years, it gave the Hansen boys considerable pleasure to notice that their aunt, Neta, was raising six boys of her own, and none of them were wearing bib overalls either.

Sometime in 1952, Neta had to leave her mission work and return to Duchess to care for her mother, Justina, who had to undergo surgery that resulted in the removal of one kidney due to cancerous growth.

While in the west, she renewed her acquaintance with John ("Jack") Broadfoot, who by this time was in his thirties and was looking for a wife like Neta. Young Esther had never seen such a huge man before. He did stand at six feet four inches in his socks. She figured that Jack was the best thing that ever happened to Neta.

Neta never did get back to the work in Toronto. She and Jack got married on December 30, 1953. They settled on his father's farm near Watrous, Saskatchewan, where they kept beef cattle and grew grain.

There they raised six huge sons, the shortest of which was as tall as his dad. They were David, Andrew, Rodrick, Kenneth, Donovan, and Lawrence. They attended the Mennonite Brethren Church which was nearby. This big family of tall people squeezed into the little pioneer shack in which Jack's folks raised their children. Only now the house was forty or fifty years older and was in a serious state of decay.

David was critically injured at age fourteen when a tractor overturned crushing his head. He was in a coma for several weeks while people everywhere, who knew the family, prayed for him. He finally recovered but was permanently damaged with a partial paralysis of one side of his face that left one eye and one ear not functioning normally.

That accident changed his life completely. He helped around home while his brothers went out to work. He was a sincere Christian and a willing helper in the church as well as in helping anyone in need or visiting the lonely. In other words, he did all the good he could for others, yet he couldn't live a completely normal life.

Most of the Broadfoot boys became what we could call "motorheads." At one time over fifty relics of car bodies in various stages of disrepair could be counted littering their yard. The boys and their dad managed to keep a fleet of old cars on the road by cannibalizing one to fix another. Occasionally they won prizes in the local stock car races.

Eventually their yard looked like and functioned like an auto wreaking company. Even Neta's house was not spared. A visitor could stumble over an engine block or an automatic transmission on his way through the porch to reach the door, or even find an engine head behind the kitchen door. One can only imagine what the boy's bedrooms must have looked like.

The whole home took on a very definite happy-go-lucky carefree masculine appearance. Jack and his sons hardly ever visited a barber, and they didn't waste a lot of time shaving either. Long hair and beards made them appear even bigger and more formidable than they really were.

Their appearance blended quite well with the context of the house and the yard they lived in, and with the patched up ancient Cadillacs they preferred to drive, and the stock car racing, and the generally carefree lifestyle they chose to live. They became a unique bunch on their block!

Yet, behind all the long hair and the unkempt beards, one could find the nicest, kindest, most helpful, thoughtful, caring men anyone could imagine. A lesson for all; one should never stereotype or pre-judge a person by his outward appearance! It is always what is inside, that counts!

Hedy Serves as Caregiver to Indigenous People

After leaving school, Hedy performed domestic service for several years for the Sam Martin and Clarence Ramer families. Then she left home to attend the Ontario Mennonite Bible School (OMBS) in January of 1948. After finishing OMBS, she worked for some time at the Braeside Home for the elderly in Preston. She returned to Alberta in August of 1949 where she worked for the Wenger family in Duchess for some time. Then she worked in mission activities among the indigenous peoples in various places including residential schools for indigenous children at St. Albert, Morley, and Whitehorse.

Hedy enrolled in a training course for Nursing Assistants in Calgary in the fall of 1959. She graduated in September 1960. For the next ten years she worked in hospitals at Gliechen, Athabasca, Wetaskiwin, and Peace River. In 1970 she went back to work at the hospital at Gliechen. When that was closed, she transferred to the Bassano Hospital where she worked until she retired after twenty-five years of nursing in 1991.

Hedy probably did more to help her folks and family than anyone else. Besides doing her share to purchase the acreage and later to purchase the house in town, she bought a lot of the furniture, paid the taxes, bought food, fuel, and whatever else was needed. Esther recalls how wonderful it was when Hedy brought home new beds. The old straw ticks could now be history. Then she put down new inlaid linoleum on the dining and living room floors. No more slivers for bare feet. And how easy to wash and wax.

In 1957 Hedy bought her first car, a brand new Simca. She was very proud of that little car. It gave her a new sense of freedom and independence. She took a lot of trips in Alberta and Saskatchewan.

Hedy took a writing course by correspondence and found enjoyment in writing letters, travelogues of her frequent journeys, etc. She kept in touch with all her nieces and nephews and grandnieces and grandnephews by sending them short letters and birthday cards.

Tena Serves as Caregiver to Orphans and the Sick

Tena, this pretty, blue-eyed blond, was also outgoing, talkative, intelligent, and ambitious, a hard worker. After quitting school, she did housework for other people such as Bennet Torkelsons, Clarence Ramers, and Joe Martins. Then she worked at the Duchess Garage in the office as receptionist.

Tena found the atmosphere at Duchess confining and restrictive. Everybody knew everybody else's business, and people had certain expectations of her that she didn't feel she wanted to meet, and that she felt they had no right to expect of her. The people were very narrow and some of them were, in her mind, clearly hypocritical. She bore scares from bad experiences for the rest of her life. She spurned at least four proposals for marriage from conventional men in the area. She had to get away and make a life for herself.

Tena moved to Calgary and found a job with the Woods Christian Home For Boys. She enjoyed the work there for some time. Later she took training as a Nursing Assistant and got a job in a hospital in Calgary. On vacations, Tena usually came home to see her family. In 1957 she bought her first car, a beautiful two-toned green 1954 Plymouth.

Tena was a dreamer, a planner, and an implementer. Whenever she came home, Tena came like a storm blowing in off the prairie, stirring up the dust and quietness as it comes. She would mobilize her family to houseclean, redecorate, or whatever. And if a sister had other ideas or was of a differing opinion, watch out! There would be confrontation. She would come in and work like mad, get the job finished and then leave just as quickly, and everything would return to its normal quiet pace.

Tena was always happy, cheerful, intense, always believing intensely in what she was doing. She was not a good listener. She didn't have time for that. It had to be along her lines, or she wasn't interested. She was very devoted to her mother and to her younger brothers and sisters. She often quarreled with her older sisters who held to more traditional and conventional ways of thinking and living.

Tena had a bad car accident. Her face was smashed. They had to wire it together. Then she was found to have cancer and had a radical mastectomy.

The operation and the trauma of going through this experience drained her of strength, making it impossible to continue with a hospital career, so she parked her car along a street in Calgary, and bought a ticket and traveled east. For three months she traveled around in the Maritime Provinces, Quebec, and Ontario. She even found a job there in a hospital for some few weeks. When she came back to Calgary, she found her car still sitting where she had abandoned it, covered with a thick layer of dust and a few leaves.

Looking for a new career, Tena moved to Ottawa, Ontario, where she took training in Library Science, and worked in a government library. She loved to study and took a keen interest in the arts and current events. She took up painting as a hobby. She undertook to write her own Memoirs, a two hundred and eighty-five pages of unpublished manuscript.

Tena took several major trips. Once she bought a "See America" bus pass for ninety-nine dollars that allowed her to travel all over the U.S.A. for one month. Twice she took a guided bus tour in Europe.

The last tour was when she was dying from cancer. By this time, she had been off work due to disability. She was taking heavy medication. She decided there was nothing to lose. She may as well sign up for the tour. She told the driver that she was sick and would just take it easy. If she felt up to it, she would get out of the bus and follow the group, and if she felt too exhausted, she would just stay on the bus and rest. If she died, well, that wouldn't be her problem, would it? She had a wonderful trip!

Helen Marries a Farmer

Helen began to work for Elizabeth and Jens in the summer of 1947 and again in the summer of 1948. She helped with milking cows, feeding pigs, haying, cutting grain, housework, and taking care of the four boys. Helen was always a cheerful happy willing helper. She was fun to be with. She loved the kids, and always saw the funny side of things.

Helen met Mervin Biehn in November of 1946 at the Mennonite's annual Christian Worker's Conference at Carstairs, Alberta. His interest was aroused, and they became better acquainted while attending a three-week Winter Bible School at Tofield which followed. They began a friendly correspondence.

Then, when Jake and Wilma were married at the Sharon Mennonite Church near Guernsey on November 16, 1947, Helen and Mervin were among their attendants. After this encounter, Mervin made sure he was present for the Summer Conference when it was held at Duchess in July of 1948. And of course, he stayed at Hansen's place where Helen was working. Their love for each other deepened.

Mervin was a farmer from Guernsey, Saskatchewan, a serious Christian, and a member of the church there. He was tall and dark and considered "handsome" by all the admiring ladies. Helen felt flattered that he would choose her above all the rest. Perhaps the man just showed good sense. In fact, those who knew Helen thought he was quite lucky to get her.

It was on a warm sunny November Sunday morning that Helen and Mervin came together at the Duchess Mennonite Church to be married. The service began, and the bride and groom were standing before the officiating minister. A strange look came over the elderly Henry B. Ramer's face. He had forgotten his little black book with the order of service and the vows in it!

Momentarily nonplussed, he quickly regained his composure, and relying on his many years of experience, went ahead and winged the whole ceremony from memory. He must have done okay, for the union lasted for forty-seven years!

There was a reception for the newlyweds afterwards, in the Friesen home. The little house was packed with friends and neighbors who came to wish them well.

After a short honeymoon in Calgary and Banff, the happy couple moved to his home in Guernsey where they took over his parent's farm in the spring of 1949. There they lived and farmed and raised their family until 1966 when they moved to Ontario.

In the early sixties a large potash company moved into the Guernsey area and bought up many of the farms, including the farms of the three Biehn families. They could stay and rent their land from the company and continue farming if they so choose.

But in 1966 they all decided to move to Ontario. Mervin bought a farm near Moorefield, to which he moved his family, livestock, and machinery. At this time, their family consisted of five children: Roy, Bernice, Edwin, Vernon, and Myron. Since then, another son, Laverne, was added.

Melita and John Plant a Grove

In the summer of 1948, an adventurous young man, John Grove, or "Johnny" as he was called, left his home in Markham, Ontario, in answer to the call, still popular in the east: "Go west young man!" He came to see the world, or at least a little different spot of it. As a lot of young men from Ontario did in those days, Johnny came to work in the harvest around Duchess.

He got acquainted with the people, especially the young people connected to the Duchess Church. Melita seemed to have that special touch that set herself apart from all the other interested and interesting available beauties, so Johnny became a frequent visitor at the Friesen home.

That winter of 1948, after the Hansen family moved to Ontario, John drove their Jeep to Ontario for them. But he couldn't stay in Ontario, the spell that the sly Melita had cast on him was irreversible and irrevocable.

On October 15, 1950, they were married in Duchess, and the happy pair settled into a little house on an acreage nearby. There they planted a new "Grove," a significant branch of the Friesen family tree. To them were born Gordon, Albert, Joe, Tom, and Debra.

John worked in the Duchess Garage for many years as a truck driver, mechanic, assembler of machinery, parts man, and troubleshooter. Eventually he went out on his own and tried farming and other odd jobs but excelled in building.

Anita Renders Domestic Service

Anita is the Friesen girl who, when swimming in the canal near their house, dived straight into the shallow water, and got her head stuck in the mud at the bottom. She wiggled and kicked her feet in the air, trying to get loose, until her sisters finally realized that she must be in distress, and slowly came to her rescue. She learned the importance of fresh air in a deeper more meaningful way that day; also, the lesson: "Look before you leap!"

Another lesson she won't forget easily is to "Look before you drink!" For one night the little girl got up in the dark to get a drink. There were no electric switches to turn on in those days, so she felt her way quietly to the dark empty kitchen to where the water pail with the dipper stood on its stand. She scooped up a dipper full of water and put it to her lips to drink.

But wait a minute, what was that furry solid thing she felt touching her lips? She hesitated, then slowly investigated with her fingers. Then she screamed. It was a drowned mouse!

There was a time when she had to skip every second day of school, because she had to share her one dress with sister Annie on alternate days, until another dress could be made.

Anita was a pretty, blond little girl, and eventually grew up to be a pretty, little blond woman. She travelled with her sister Elizabeth's family to Ontario, in the fall of 1948, to help them get settled into their new home. She helped them on the farm until August of 1949, when she returned to Alberta with her sister Hedy.

Back in Alberta, she received a kick on the head from a horse. That kick was almost fatal. She was hospitalized with a bad concussion for some time. For many years after that, Anita was bothered by severe headaches and occasional seizures that were considered epileptic. She did housework for a lot of different people.

In the late 1950's, Anita went to Bible School at Briercrest in Saskatchewan for several winters. There she met and brought home a fine

Englishman that some of her nephews were sure would add some variety to the motley collection of uncles that was growing, but it wasn't to be.

In 1960, she settled for a local boy, when she married the carpenter, Jake Dyck, in a nice ceremony at the Immanuel Assembly. They made their home in Brooks. In 1962, they adopted the pretty little baby, Connie Lea. In 1965 they added a baby boy, Glen Robert.

Annie and Lyle Establish a Family in Tofield

Annie graduated from the Brooks High School in 1951. She was the first of the Friesen family to go that far in education. That fall she signed up for her first real job at the Indian Residential School near St. Albert where her sister Hedy was working. They both lived in the residence and worked in the various departments of the school. One weekend they took a bus to visit their brother and sister, Jake and Wilma and family at Smith, Alberta. They were met by Jake at the depot with a two wheeled horse-drawn cart.

Annie felt homesickness and didn't adjust to her job very well. She describes how she left it:

> *I soon knew this job was not for me. I was unmatched for what might have been a very different kind of life.*
>
> *One lovely fall evening I strolled across the yard to the residence of the administrator to give my notice. He was sick in bed. However, his wife invited me in and served tea. They were world travelers and had a very white polar bear rug on the floor with its mouth open wide. They were very kind and sympathetic; said they were expecting it.*
>
> *The maintenance person took me along to Edmonton to the train station. He was very kind, shook my hand, and wished me well.*
>
> *I then looked around the crowded station for a place to sit feeling alone and somewhat lost. There was a seat between a man and lady. The man saw my label on the suitcase and spoke to me of someone he knew in Duchess. The lady said to me "You are a Christian, I can tell!" She was a missionary en route to Africa. I sure was happy for her company* (Annie Roth, a letter, 1993).

When Annie reached home, she found her mother was in the hospital, having had a gall bladder operation.

The following winter, Annie traveled to Tofield to attend a winter Bible School for six weeks at the Salem Mennonite Church. She did some part-time housekeeping to pay her expenses. It was there that she met her tall, dark, and handsome, the youthful Lyle Roth. A romance budded which soon blossomed into a marriage which was solemnized at the Duchess Mennonite Church on November 12, 1953. After honeymooning in Banff, they settled in the Tofield area.

In those days, the homes in the rural areas didn't have natural gas nor electricity. The Roths cut wood in the bush or hauled coal by horse and wagon or sleigh from the mine seven miles away to heat their home. Coal was shoveled by hand into the basement and ashes carried out by bucket. Water was carried in by pail. Coal oil lamps, lanterns, and gas lamps supplied the light at night. The outdoor privy accommodated the call of nature in daylight and in darkness, in smelly, fly-infested heat of summer and in the bone-chilling cold of winter. Rural electrification came in 1955, and natural gas service reached them in 1974.

The newlyweds had very little money in those days, but bought their first car, a 1947 Mercury. Annie learned to drive in it. In those days people learned by doing. They never bothered about drivers courses, driver's tests, licenses, nor insurance. It wasn't till 1963 that she had to bother about those things.

Arthur Lyle was born on November 23, 1954. That winter the family moved to the "Blackburn place," a farm they rented which had a big, cold, and drafty house. Lyle worked the night shift at the Dodds coal mine. He also cut brush along the roadways for the county. Annie took care of baby Arthur, the house, and the few cows they milked. On May 3, 1956, Curtis Ray was born.

It came time to get a better car, so they bought a red and white coupe. It didn't start very well in winter. One Sunday morning it refused to start, so they hooked up the team of horses to pull-start it. Annie sat on the hood to drive the horses, while Lyle sat inside to regulate the levers to keep it going, if it ever started.

A neighbor drove by, and Annie was embarrassed. Just think of how it must have looked – Annie, dressed in her finest Sunday regalia, sitting, straddling the icy cold car hood, clinging to the horses' reins, urging them to "Go faster, faster!" while desperately trying to keep from sliding off the shiny hood, and her man sitting comfortably in the car doing basically nothing! Eventually, they did get the car to start.

In the summer of 1957, Lyle got a job in Tofield at Arnett Motors. He also drove school bus to supplement their income. They rented a house in Tofield. Now they had electricity and gas but no water and sewer.

In 1958, while working in the garage, an improperly blocked vehicle fell on Lyle and smashed his leg. It could so easily have been fatal. He went on workers' compensation for most of a year while his leg slowly mended. He was left with a permanent limp.

Working on the concrete floor all day, with the bad leg, was too difficult, so Lyle quit. He got another job working for Boyd Stauffer on his farm, where they were given a little house in which to live. Their firstborn, Arthur, started school from there.

That year, their second son, Curtis, became very sick and needed blood transfusions. The cause confused the doctors. After a lot of testing, specialists finally diagnosed that he had Gauche disease, a very rare disease of unknown cause, and no cure, and no effective treatment. The specialists of that era did not give much hope that he would live long or enjoy a normal life.

The young boy, Curtis, became very familiar with hospitals, spending many months at a time, several times through those early years. Yet, he kept a positive attitude and never gave up the struggle. He managed to carry on okay in school and did light work as he grew up.

During his long hospitalizations, he cooperated with the researching doctors as a "guinea pig," giving himself as an object upon which to experiment and test medications in their efforts to learn about and find a treatment or cure for this rare disease. Due to progress made, Curtis eventually was able to marry and fathered two children and held good responsible jobs that supported his family.

After the Curtis' birth, Lyle took a job driving the local bread truck and the family moved to Ryley. Victor Lee was born on May 3, 1962, and Verlene Kay on November 24, 1964. The family moved to Camrose in 1965 where Lyle worked for Crawford & Co. driving truck and setting up machinery for the next nine years. Robin Stewart was born on May 23, 1968.

Edward Establishes a Career

Every fall the Friesen children took a few weeks off from school to earn a little money picking potatoes for neighboring farmers. Ed recalls being "not much taller than a 100 lb. sack of potatoes," when he started in the tradition of his elder siblings. Sometimes his big sisters helped finish his row, putting the potatoes in his sack, boosting his income. He used his money to buy schoolbooks and clothes. He recalls:

> *When I bought my sheepskin lined parka, I was the envy of my friends. I would never be cold again. Then I bought moccasins with felt liners and now even deep snow couldn't stop me.... Another purchase I made was a pair of rebuilt army boots which weighed 4½ pounds with one-inch soles, steel plates under heels and toes. I could make sparks with the heels on cement. Mom never liked them. Once I rode bareback to Hansen's with these boots on. My legs must have stretched 4½ inches. They seemed to disappear one day, and I think Mom must have buried them deep in the garden* (A letter from Edward Friesen, 1993).

In January of 1950, Ed was diagnosed as having rheumatic fever. He spent the next two months in the hospital in Brooks. Recovery was slow, resulting in his missing school for one and one-half years. In September of 1951, he was able to return to grade nine. Esther and David also fell ill with rheumatic fever.

Edward took his last year of school at Rosemary, finishing grade eleven in 1954. He did odd jobs in the area that summer and purchased his first wheels, a 1939 half-ton Chevrolet truck for the very low price of ninety dollars! He was very proud of that truck!

For three months that fall, Ed worked for Lauver's, a bulk fuel agent in Duchess, delivering fuel to farmers. Then he got a job trucking and stacking hay for John Martin. In April 1956, Ed started working for the Eastern Irrigation District as a dragline helper and operator in-training in the summer months, and on construction during the winter months. The construction was a lot of four-pound hammer and six-inch spike kind of work. He recalls:

> *One cold winter day we were mixing and pouring concrete for a big canal water gate. A storm came up with a sudden drop in temperature. There was nothing to stop the cold prairie wind. Since it was a huge structure, we had to complete the pouring of concrete. We could barely keep the gravel and water warm enough to keep from freezing while mixing the concrete. Bigger batches of concrete had to be mixed and wheelbarrows had to be filled fuller using two men instead of one to pull the wheelbarrows up the ramp. By the time we were up, it took two men again to dump the wheelbarrows. Fortunately, no one had a weak heart, but there were wobbly knees!* (a letter from Edward Friesen, 1993).

Ed switched jobs again in August 1957. This time he worked for the Duchess Garage as a truck driver hauling cattle and machinery. He enjoyed this adventure very much. He enjoyed going places and meeting people. He was proud of the new turquoise green Fargo and long semi-trailer cattle liner. However, after two years, he got to thinking that he might not want to be single or to drive truck all his life. So, he signed up to become an apprentice mechanic at the Duchess Garage. He worked at that for four years, attending classes at the Southern Alberta Institute of Technology in Calgary for two months each year. He received his Mechanic's License in March of 1963.

Ed's '39 Chev truck soon gave way to a '52 Plymouth sedan, as that was much more practical for a large family in which his was the only reliable means of transportation. Ed helped his parents a lot with transportation, putting food on the table, and supplying fuel for the winter. He helped his younger brother and sisters, who were still in school, with their needs in so many ways.

Ed was a very hard worker, went out of his way to be helpful to anyone in need, was always laughing his way through any hardship or crisis, was forever talking, telling stories, cracking jokes, and laughing at them himself. His wit was only matched with his wisdom. He exhibited a remarkable degree of good common sense. His presence was always an asset in any group setting. People appreciated and respected Ed.

The "Brotherhood of Bachelors, Local 977"

Edward Friesen, Peter Hansen, and Doug Schindelier struck up a strong friendship in 1957 that lasted until they all got married. Edward was the oldest. He considered himself a seasoned bachelor, having dated only one girl once way back in 1954. He boasted of "four years of clean living!" These three became inseparable friends. They formed what they called "The Brotherhood Of Bachelors, Local 977."

All three of them had a good sense of humor, but each one's humor was unique to him. Doug could be very formal and almost pompous. His humor was so dry that it was almost brittle. People, who didn't know him, often took him seriously and really couldn't figure him out. Yet he would say the funniest things in the funniest way.

Ed was the opposite. His sense of humor spilled out all over. It oozed from his countenance; his face was always lit up with a smile. He was the first to laugh at his own jokes, which were numerous and frequent. People didn't know if he was ever serious. Sometimes they laughed along with him, more because of him than at his jokes.

Peter's sense of humor expressed itself in the exaggerated way he used big words and in the apparent seriousness with which he used hyperbole, irony, and cynicism.

For a while, if they were not on their jobs, these three could always be found doing things together. They would work on their cars together, go traveling together, socialize around the local coffee shops, but mostly visit around one of their homes together—often into the wee hours of the morning. Friendship can be a beautiful thing!

The first cracks appeared in the solidarity of the Brotherhood during the Annual Conference, hosted by the Duchess Mennonite Church in 1958. Doug and Peter violated the guidelines of the Brotherhood by having dates. This was a serious threat at first. However, the distance of the girls from the guys signaled a possible safety factor.

Then the "Dear John" letters saved Local 977 from early dissolution. Although, shaken and a bit wobbly, the Brotherhood survived intact until 1962, when Doug moved away, and Ed and Peter both got involved in serious courtship that led to engagement and ultimately to marriage in 1964.

As a byproduct of those two almost fatal dates, Doug had lured Edward into initiating a relationship with a girl near Guernsey, Saskatchewan. Just that quickly, Doug lost his welcome there, so Ed had no one to keep him company on the next long, lonely journey he had to make to see his love. So, he recruited his nephew, Carl for this task.

And Carl, being eager to please his superiors, and always curious to visit new territory, fell for it. Of course, Ed dipped the "carrot" in a little "honey" by enticing him with the promise that his girlfriend had a beautiful younger sister that would undoubtably be of considerable interest to him. Carl, ever the adventurer, was very willing to explore the possibilities.

An opportunity opened in the spring of 1960, when Ed got a long weekend off from duties in the garage. They left in the evening after work and drove the whole night, covering the 400 plus miles to Guernsey, arriving about four a.m. at Ed's sister, Helen, and Mervin Biehn's place. They had a very warm welcome and a nice visit there and enjoyed playing with Helen's four rambunctious kids.

Finally, the time came for Carl to meet the sister that Ed had been bragging up. Yes, she was everything he promised and much more beside! She was only fifteen years old at the time, young and innocent, and very pretty. Yet she acted very mature and had a good sense of humor. They were both shy, but with uncle's help, soon became friends.

Everyone thought that Ed and his love would certainly marry in the near future; but then suddenly, they broke off the relationship. Edward, disappointed, re-instated himself into the roster of membership and reluctantly accepted the high standards required of the single life in "The Brotherhood, Local 977."

However, Ed found that re-couped status to be disappointing, a dead end, leading nowhere. In August of 1962, he started a courting relationship with Faye Roth, the eldest daughter of Joe and Fern Roth of Tofield, Alberta. He was deeply impressed with the qualities he found in her, all he ever hoped to find in a girl. The "Brotherhood" was dead!

However, Faye had already signed up for a voluntary service assignment with the denomination's Mission Board in Elkhart, Indiana. There were delays in the processing of her assignment, so Ed "made hay while the sun shone" and bonds of friendship deepened, and they grew close to each other. They sought the Lord's guidance.

Then Faye received her call to Elkhart, and Ed received a call by his Church to move to Eaglesham, Alberta, to help with the Church work there. He would support himself by working in Lloyd King's garage. So, they parted ways in opposite directions for a time.

In May of 1964, Faye received an early release from her assignment with the Mission Board and came home. She and Ed were married the next month on June 26th. The happy couple made their first home in Eaglesham. There Patty Jo was born a year later.

Things did not go so well at Eaglesham, so the three moved to Fairview in December of 1966. There they bought a house. Ed worked as mechanic at the Ford garage for some years. Then he worked for the Fairview School Division, three years as a school bus mechanic, and four years as a supervisor. Sherilyn Fern joined the family on June 11, 1967, and the arrival of Kenton Edward completed the "Friesen Five" on November 20, 1968.

Susan Serves in the Secretarial World

Susan was a meticulous and careful clean person. She moved to Ontario in the mid 1950's and worked for several evangelical organizations, including Ken Campbell Crusade's. She lived in a small private apartment in Kitchener. For many years, she worked in the Sir Wilfred Laurier University as a secretary, assisting in the writing and publishing of documents. She suffered from delicate health issues in her later years.

Martha Builds Her Nest in Ontario

Martha was a missionary at heart. When she got her first job away from home, she used her tithe money to adopt a Korean orphan through one of those agencies. She supported him until he grew up. Later, after marriage, she and her husband were involved with supporting a children's hospital in Haiti for many years.

Albert Grove, the younger brother to John Grove had traveled from his home in Ontario to Alberta to visit John and Melita and family, and "to see the world." He had stayed on for a while getting a little work here and there and making a few friends.

One of those few friends he made was Melita's sister, Martha. Now Martha was, at age eighteen, the prettiest girl, not only in the whole Friesen family of eleven girls, but in the entire church! And of course, Albert, at age twenty, was the most "tall, dark, and handsome" stranger that Martha had ever set eyes upon!

Of course, when it was time for Albert to return to his home in Ontario, Martha and her older sister, Susan, felt it would be proper to follow their older sisters' footsteps to Ontario to attend the Ontario Mennonite Bible School. That was in the fall of 1955. So, there was a wedding in 1956 at Duchess.

The happy couple settled down near the town of Hanover in Ontario. Albert worked as a carpenter, became a draftsman and builder, then a contractor, and years later got involved with a consortium of three other men who ran group homes for children, the handicapped, and for the aged. The couple had three children, Jerry, Marianne, and Valerie.

Jerry was killed instantly by a car which struck him while riding his bicycle on a quiet country road one foggy morning in July of 1975. It was a great shock to all the family, but especially to his parents.

The marriage relationship, that started with so much romance and so much promise, was undergoing a period of stress at the time when Jerry was killed. After this blow, the marriage slowly disintegrated. Albert found companionship with someone else, and Martha lived alone for several years.

Esther Begins a Life of Caregiving

After Esther Friesen quit high school in 1961, she took Nursing Assistant's training for ten months and graduated in 1962. She worked in the Medicine Hat General Hospital for six months. She missed her family and her church, so when an opportunity opened to work at the Brooks Hospital, she jumped for the chance.

Her brother, David, had enrolled in the Ontario Mennonite Bible Institute in the fall of 1961. He would be returning for the five-month course each winter for three years. Esther decided to attend the three-month Bible School from January through March. She arranged with the Brooks Hospital for the three months leave each winter and started going to the Ontario Mennonite Bible School in January of 1964. She graduated in the spring of 1966.

After graduation, Esther worked in the hospital on the Gliechen Indian Reservation. She worked until June, then returned to Ontario to volunteer at the Frazer Lake Camp for ten weeks as a camp nurse, counsellor, and laundry worker. She enjoyed this ministry. In the fall she took a job as cook at the Bible Institute in Kitchener. Although she missed nursing, she needed the social life she found in that setting. For Christmas break, Esther went to visit her brother, David, who by now was married to Esther Derstine and was living in Evanston, Illinois. There she received word that her mother was ill.

She returned to her work in Ontario, but in mid-January of 1967, went home to see her mother. She found her terminally ill with cancer, but not at an advanced stage yet. Her mother urged her to return to finish her job which would end in April. After completing her job, Esther returned to Duchess and took care of her mother for the last five months of her final illness.

David Deserts to the USA

David Friesen was the second of the fourteen Friesen children to graduate from high school, and the first to matriculate at the top of his class. That was in June of 1961. He was a math and physics whiz. He was socially well adjusted and was liked by everybody. Like his brother, Ed, he enjoyed telling funny stories, and enjoyed even more laughing at them himself.

Being the fourteenth and last child in the home, he received less discipline and more pampering than any of his siblings. In fact, life had less hardships for him than any of the others. Yet he was not spoiled in any sense. He was very responsible and appreciated all the opportunities he had.

After graduating from Duchess High School, David worked at a summer job in the Dinosaur Park. Then he went to the Ontario Mennonite Bible Institute in Kitchener, Ontario, for five winter months each year for the next three years. He apprenticed with Bev Hutchinson, a Certified Public Accountant in Brooks, during the seven-month break between Bible Institute terms. He continued working with Hutchinson after he graduated in the spring of 1964.

Sometimes those Bible Schools were called "match factories", and not without some justification. For many a match was made in those sacred halls between "light-foot lads and rose-lipped maidens"!

And David was no exception, for he met his match there too in the indomitable, yet kind, and gentle Esther Derstine from Lansdale, Pennsylvania. They decided on marriage the following year.

But Esther was not about to leave the love and warmth of home, and the security of her civilized and affluent community in eastern Pennsylvania, for the harsh and unpredictable wilds of western Canada; and David, knowing too well the story of the struggles of his family, couldn't raise a reasonable objection to her position. So, he swallowed whatever remained of the vain patriotism he may have felt, and prepared to migrate to the U.S.A.

In August of 1965, the happy couple were united in holy matrimony in Lansdale, Pennsylvania. David held a job with a local bakery, a legal front to meet the requirements for immigration. He soon found a job with an accounting firm and was enjoying the prospects of apprenticing again for his chosen career.

But then Uncle Sam called. This ex-Canadian, recent immigrant wasn't going to get away with hiding behind his wife's skirts, while other native sons were fighting and dying in Viet Nam to "keep America free"! The newlywed would have to answer the "call" of his adopted country!

David, having registered as a "CO", was sent to work in a hospital in Evanston, Illinois for two years. That was the uncalculated cost of his moving to the U.S.A.

Slowing Down

As Jacob and Justina got older, less, and less of the activities revolved around them, and more and more of the action revolved around their growing children. By the mid-fifties, the older children had abandoned the nest and spread out in every direction to seek their careers, and some of them found their mates and started nests of their own. The youngest were to finish their high school years with the decade.

When Jens and Elizabeth moved their family back from Ontario it was possible to have the first Friesen Family Reunion at Duchess in the summer of 1956. A head count at that time indicated that the family had grown to forty-two in number.

In the late 1950's Jacob Friesen gave up farming altogether. He had always been a part-time farmer, finding temporary employment away from home as a carpenter, laborer, handyman, or whatever. Now he would go into that kind of employment full-time.

He never stuck to one job very long. He was always restless, finding something that didn't suit him about the job, the working conditions, the boss, or the wages. There was always a good reason to move on.

One summer he got an easy government job operating the McGregory ferry. He kept that job for several months, but that too had some undesirable conditions, and he disappointed his family by quitting. Sometimes one wonders if he wasn't a genius, misplaced by history and circumstances?

When they reached age sixty-five, Jacob and Justina both retired on the government old-age pension. They were used to living on little, and now they were very happy and able to retire on little!

Jacob & Justina Friesen Family Reunion – Summer 1956

12

Settling into Utopia at Last

Then Abraham breathed his last and died at a good old age, an old man and full of years; and he was gathered to his people. His sons Isaac and Ishmael buried him in the cave of Machpelah near Mamre. – Genesis 25:8, 9

In 1963, Hedy sold the ten-acre farm, which had been home for her folks for so many years and purchased the small Godfrey house in the town of Duchess. At last, her parents would have the luxury of electric lights, gas heating, hot and cold running water, and a telephone.

Now, receiving a government pension, they could retire in dignity and comfort. The times of hard labor, sacrificing, and suffering the indignities of poverty were finally over. The luxuries were overwhelming. Justina facetiously remarked to a daughter "We'll have to pray that we don't get worldly!" "But" she admitted, "it is not hard to get used to something better!"

Jake Friesen was living in Duchess at the time and allowed his dad to build a shack on his land so he would have a place to store his tools and to do the tinkering that he loved so much to do.

Although Jacob Friesen always had a healthy appetite, his health was not so good. He struggled with overweight. Well, he didn't "struggle", that was the problem. He would eat and gain weight until he reached about 260 lbs. His blood pressure would go way up, and he would get sick until he needed to be hospitalized. There a stringent diet would be imposed until he lost forty or fifty pounds, after which he would feel better and would be discharged.

After some months he would regain the excess weight and get sick again. The hospital treatment would be repeated. Doctors warned him, that he was liable to have a stroke if that condition persisted.

Justina Friesen had lived a long and hard life. In 1952 when she was fifty-five years of age, it was discovered that she had cancer in one of her kidneys. She prayed, asking God to spare her life until her children wouldn't need her anymore. David, her youngest was about ten years of age at that time. She spent most of that summer in the Calgary General Hospital where the doctors had operated, removing the infected kidney. God heard her prayer, and she had enjoyed another fifteen years of reasonably good health.

Before Christmas of 1966, she had painted the basement walls and floor of their new house. She had entertained Ed and Faye over the Christmas holiday. But now in January of 1967, she wasn't feeling well at all, being hardly able to walk, and Melita persuaded her to see a doctor. She was admitted to the Brooks Hospital.

Justina was seventy years old by this time. Her many years of suffering and hard labor had taken their toll. The doctors said that she had a body of an eighty-year-old, worn out. Her life's work was completed.

Melita wrote a letter to Esther who was working in Ontario indicating that the end was near. If anyone wanted to say "Goodbye!" they should come soon. Esther took two weeks off from work and came home.

David and his wife, Esther, also heard the alarming news while living in Evanston. He contacted Carl Hansen, who was studying in Virginia at Eastern Mennonite College, and invited him and his wife, Vera, to join them on a trip to visit his mother in Alberta.

So, Carl and Vera and baby Cindy took a train to Chicago, where David met them. From there they set out together, by car, for Alberta. They drove the 1700 wintry miles straight through, non-stop, to Duchess.

They found Mother Friesen resting in the Brooks General Hospital. She was not well, but she was not in a critical condition either. The doctors avoided the word "cancer." They were very vague about the nature of her illness, what it was, what could be done to treat it, or what we could expect to come of it.

Finally, they indicated there was nothing they could do for her except to keep her as comfortable as possible and warned the family that she should not be expected to recover. Much later the doctors admitted that they thought she was full of cancer, including cancer of the bones.

After Esther returned to Ontario, David took his mother home from the hospital, at her request. She wanted to die at home without "heroic measures" to prolong her sufferings. Davids and Carls would return to the United States, and Jacob would care for his wife at home.

When she returned home, Justina and Jacob were alone for a few weeks. They talked and shared like they seldom did before in light of these final realities. Jacob made his peace with God. They prayed together. They had a German record that had a song on it called "I'll Be No Stranger There." He played it over and over. It was a blessed time for both. Yet she was not getting better. She only attended Church once; her last time to do so.

A few weeks later, on a Saturday morning in February, Jacob went, as usual, to get the mail. The Post Office was only half a block away. He never returned.

Justina was still able to walk around with difficulty. So, she went and sat by the kitchen window and waited. Some hours later, her son, Jake, came and told her that his dad was in the Brooks General Hospital. He had had a bad stroke downtown. Someone had found him lying in the snow and called Jake, who rushed him to the hospital.

The stroke left him permanently paralyzed on one side and with reduced mental capacities. He would never live at home nor help himself again. He was sixty-eight years of age at that time. The doctors said he could live in this condition for as long as seven years. Little did they know that he would live under nursing care for the next eighteen years!

Justina was able to go in and visit him at the hospital once. That was the last time they were together on this earth.

Jacob Friesen was transferred to the Medicine Hat Auxiliary Hospital where he stayed for several years until 1971, when the Newell Nursing Home was built in Brooks. Under nursing care, he lost all his excess weight.

He regained some, but not all, of his mental powers and would say the most outlandish things. When someone visited him the following summer, he told them that he just got back from a trip to the moon. That person joked along with him and said, "I heard it was made of green cheese!" He said, "No, it is made of plywood!" So that settled that question until the Apollo mission reached it about a year later and cast some doubt upon his findings.

Sheri Friesen remembers when she and her sister and brother went to visit their grandfather and proceeded to sing "Gott ist die Liebe" for him, in German and in English. Afterwards, he said that was the first time he had heard that song in English.

Melita Grove moved in with her mother to take care of her. Her family ate their meals there but slept at home. Ontario Mennonite Bible School was over before Easter, and Esther came home right away.

Esther, traveling with David Donaldson on their way home, had a bad car accident in the middle of the night about seventy-five miles east of Medicine Hat. Esther was battered and bruised but not broken. She phoned John Grove, who came, with Lyle Roth, to pick them up at Medicine Hat. By five a.m. she was sitting in her mother's kitchen eating summer sausage and drinking coffee with Annie and Lyle. That was Easter weekend.

The Monday night after Easter, the family got a call from the Auxiliary that their dad was very ill with pneumonia, and that he was not expected to live through the night. Lyle, Annie, Jake, Wilma, and Esther rushed over to Medicine Hat to be with him. He survived that round, the first of many more rounds with pneumonia that he won in the following eighteen years.

Melita moved back home to her family, and Esther began to care for her mother at home on a fulltime basis.

Gradually Justina got worse. She could no longer walk, then she could no longer sit. The cancer was in her spine and made it very painful. Then she could no longer sit on a special commode. She ate a little soft food and soup and drank coffee.

Nurse, Marian Martin faithfully came twice a day to give her an injection of morphine or other strong pain killer. Towards the end, nothing could kill the pain.

Visitors came and went every day. They brought cheer and comfort and showed that they cared. Young people from the Bethel Church came every Wednesday night and sang her favorite songs. She appreciated this so much that she requested them to sing several songs at her funeral, which they did.

Pastors from several churches came regularly throughout the summer. Clarence later said, "We went away from visiting her feeling she had given us more then we could give her."

The Grove grandchildren took turns sleeping there to keep Esther company. They often came in and sat and visited their grandmother. She loved to be with children.

Carl and Vera had agreed to accept an assignment with the Eastern Mennonite Board of Missions and Charities (EMBMC) to teach at the Nazareth Bible Academy in Ethiopia for three years. After orientation and commissioning in Salunga, Pennsylvania, they came home with their two-year old daughter, Cindy, in August, to say "Goodbye" to their family, and to wait for the Ethiopian Government to approve their visas.

It was harvest time, and Carl was able to get involved in helping a bit. His grandmother was still living, so they visited her quite often, talked, read from the Bible, and prayed with her. She appreciated that so much.

They were waiting for their visas to be approved, so their flight dates could be finalized, and tickets issued. They waited and waited. The school, where Carl was to teach, was to open in early September. Early September came and went, but there was still no word about visas. The Mission Board told them: "Just be patient, it could be approved at any time, including a month or two later than you wish."

Justina always was one to do things properly and on time. As she lived, so in dying she was ready in every sense, even in planning her and her husband's funeral services. Esther writes:

> *One day Mom asked me to bring paper and pen to her room. She outlined all her's and Dad's funeral services and made a will of what everyone in the family should get from the home. She picked a dress to be buried in. It was the dress she made from the material David's wife's mother had given her as a gift once. Although they had never met, the gift had meant a lot to Mom.*

Justina Reaches Utopia First

On her last Wednesday, as she was slipping in and out of a coma, the young people came in and sang for her. Clarence and Ethel Ramer were sitting by her bed with several of the family members when she opened her eyes and said, "I heard the Angels sing!" Esther writes:

> *Mom went into a coma Tuesday, September 19th. Melita had come over and we were changing her bed when Mom seemed to just fade away. It was very hard even though we knew she*

would die soon, and we even prayed for her release from pain as she suffered terrible.

We called Marian Martin who was a nurse who had been coming over to give Mom medication by injection. She came right over. She stayed with me for a few hours.... Mom drifted in and out of a coma that week.... On September 22nd Mom turned seventy-one. It was a very quiet day. I was alone with her nearly all day.... Jake came to see her. Elizabeth came for the night, but we sat up all night.

Saturday, Vera, and Cindy came with Elizabeth and Freda, and Melita came over. Tom, Debra, and Freda went in to see Mom and she opened her eyes and smiled and said, "Oh, it is the children!" Later she said she saw her mother and one of her brothers.... Once she said, "They are coming for me now!" She died around five p.m. on September 23, 1967, seventy-one years and one day after she was born, she passed away quietly in peace, just as she had lived. The doctor came with the ambulance to pick up her body and said, "She has had a bad time before she died." The signs of a suffering body were all too clear.

That evening most of the local family members gathered at the house and began making funeral arrangements and making phone calls to scattered family members and others that should know. The funeral date was set for Wednesday, September 27th. Arrangements had to be made to host the family members that would come from afar.

Carl was helping dig his grandmother's grave when a phone call came from the Mission Board notifying them that the visas had been granted. They wondered what date they preferred to fly. They asked for the day after the funeral. It seemed to them that it was the hand of God in arranging the timing of the issuing of the visas to make it possible for them to be present at this awesome occasion.

Justina's funeral was conducted according to her wishes. Clarence Ramer gave the appropriate meditation. She chose scripture and songs that expressed her faith and deepest longings: "Psalms 121," "Safe In The Arms Of Jesus," "Rock of Ages," "Only A Sinner Saved By Grace," "Going

Down The Valley," "How Beautiful Heaven Must Be," "Take Thou My Hand Oh Father," (The song sung at their farewell when they left their home in Russia forty-three years earlier) "Will The Circle Be Unbroken?" "I Need No Mansion Here Below," and "There Is Sweet Rest In Heaven."

Some of these were sung as special numbers by the Torkelson young people who had visited her often and sang for her while she was bedfast. Her body was laid to rest in the Duchess Cemetery.

All of Justina's fourteen children attended her funeral. They were, from oldest to youngest: Elizabeth (Mrs. Jens Hansen) and Jacob of Duchess, Alta., Neta (Mrs. Jack Broadfoot) of Watrous, Sask., Hedy of Athabasca, Alta., Tena of Ottawa, Ont., Helen (Mrs. Mervin Biehn) of Moorefield, Ont., Melita (Mrs. John Grove) of Duchess, Alta., Anita (Mrs. Jake Dyck) of Brooks, Alta., Annie (Mrs. Lyle Roth) of Camrose, Alta., Susan of Kitchener, Ont., Edward of Fairview, Alta., Martha (Mrs. Albert Grove) of Walkerton, Ont., Esther of Duchess, Alta., and David of Evanston, Ill. She had twenty-eight grandsons, thirteen granddaughters, and three great-grand-daughters at the time of her passing.

That evening after the funeral, Carl and Vera, and some others, drove to Medicine Hat to say "Goodbye!" to their grandfather. They did not expect to see him again on this earth. They found him in good spirits. They told him that they were going to set out for Ethiopia tomorrow, and that they would be working there for a period of three years. He said, "Yes, I was there two weeks ago when I went to visit Haile Selassie." In his permanently mentally damaged state, it did not seem out of the ordinary that they should be going to that exotic place.

Esther Marries

Following the death of her mother, Esther returned to work at the Brooks Hospital almost immediately. She needed to get back on her feet financially. But she was restless. What was there in Brooks for her as far as a future was concerned? With no home nor home responsibilities, she was free to look elsewhere.

In 1970 she got a job in the High River Hospital and worked there for a year and a half. She made many new friends and enjoyed her work, yet still, she was restless. There must be something more fulfilling than this? She applied for a job at Williams Lake, B.C. and at Spirit River, Alberta. She prayed that God would open the way and direct her to the job that she was supposed to take.

While Esther waited, she was introduced, through a friend at work, to John Visser of Calgary. He was a widower with four children. Esther found this frightening. After they had met and got acquainted, John suggested that she resign from her job and come and stay with them for a while, then they could see how they felt about the possibility of their getting married.

While considering that option, letters of job acceptances came from both Williams Lake and Spirit River. Talk about answers to prayer—now she had three, and she did not know which one was the right one. To marry a man ten years older than herself, with four growing children, would not be easy. Yet the children needed a mother, and the man needed a wife. Esther had a lot of experience, caring for her many nieces and nephews and other sick children down through the years. And, well, yes, she did need a husband!

Esther struggled with her decision. John did not go to church, had not been interested in religion, and made no promise to start going now. He did promise to let Esther take the two littlest girls to church, and that he would never ask Esther to not go. At least she understood where he stood on this important difference between them.

Then one fellow at work suggested to her, "You do not want to go to Williams Lake!" She agreed, that really, deep down inside, she did not want to go there. But Spirit River wasn't that appealing either. Then she recalls, "I went to church one Sunday morning, and I really can't tell what happened, I just knew what I was supposed to do."

John and Esther were married on March 18th, 1972, in a quiet ceremony in the home of John and Melita Grove. It was not easy for Esther to move in with a family in mid-course.

Leo was a big nineteen-year-old tech student who supported himself working part time. Joan was a seventeen-year-old high school graduate who was working at her first job in a bank. She moved into her own apartment. Teresa was nine and Veronica was eight. The girls resented Esther's intrusion into their father's life and their home. It was painful for them and equally painful for Esther. There were times when Esther felt it had been a terrible mistake. Yet John was extremely kind and considerate and wanted everything to work out for them.

They lived in Calgary until 1980 when John was transferred to Edmonton. They bought a house in Sherwood Park. Teresa stayed in Calgary. Veronica moved back to Calgary two years later after finishing high school. The relationship between Esther and the stepchildren improved very slowly, but as they married and had children of their own, they all were glad to have a grandmother and grandfather in Edmonton.

Esther gave of her free time to volunteer work. For seven years she was a Brownie leader. She took a course and then served in the Shelter for battered women and children for six months. She took another course under the Pastoral Care program at the General Hospital and did volunteer work on the Palliative Care ward. Then she took a refresher course and returned to work as a Nursing Assistant in 1986. For two and one-half years she worked for the Edmonton Medical Registry. She did private duty and worked on the wards in many city hospitals and institutions. In 1989 she was hired by the University Hospital in a float pool as relief person.

John and Esther got along well. John provided a place to call home, gave her security and stability and provided a sense of identity that she needed. Esther helped John to step out a lot socially. They were very good for each other. She traveled with him to Holland several times and got to know his family.

The Passing of Uncle John

Years after the Hansen family returned from Ontario, John Warkentin would go around about twice a year to visit them. He was always happy to see them, and they would welcome him in, serve coffee, and listen to him for a while. Then Jens would invite him to stay for supper, give some excuse to get out of the house and go about his work. The evening would be plenty long to listen to his stories.

His English was not the best, and he mumbled quite a bit. That was one reason his stories seldom made sense to the listeners. He was so cynical and negative, one soon felt dirty just hearing him talk. There was no use for the kids nor even Jens to argue with him, so they would just endure and let him run on and on. They always prepared a bed for him.

The next morning, he would have a leisurely breakfast. He would sit hunched over, with his elbow resting on the table, holding a slice of bread in his flat upturned palm at eye level, slowly spreading the butter, with a knife in the other hand, and all the while talking slowly. Around ten o'clock, he would say his farewells, and slowly shuffle out, and finally get into his ancient car, and make his slow departure.

Uncle John's health began to fail. In 1970 he had a kidney removed in the Brooks Hospital, after which he no longer felt able to make the long drive to Borden, Saskatchewan. A year later, he was hospitalized again. After surgery in the Foothills hospital in Calgary, he was transferred to the hospital in Bassano for recouperation. Later, he was transferred to the hospital in Brooks, where he died on February 8th, 1972.

After his death, an autopsy was performed. He was found to have cancer on his brain. One wonders how long the cancer was there, and if it might have had something to do with the way he lived?

John Warkentin was the only uncle the fourteen Friesen children ever knew.

Jacob Reaches Utopia at Last

For almost eighteen years Jacob lingered on in the Auxiliary Hospital, first in Medicine Hat and then, when a new facility was opened, in Brooks. Although his stroke damage was permanent, the carefully controlled diet and excellent health care kept him in good condition. He had lost all excess weight and the danger of recurring strokes was sleight. So, he just lingered there and aged ever so slowly. At times he would have a bout with pneumonia, but with medication, his strong constitution always rallied.

But as it does to all human flesh, eventually time wore him down. In June of 1985, in his eighty-seventh year, the ravages of time finally overcame this sturdy pioneer. On June 11, his children were notified that they should come if they wished to say, "Goodbye!" Some of the children arrived on time to be with him before he slipped away. Annie and Lyle, Esther and John, and the local ones took turns keeping vigil. Jake and Wilma were already on their way from Ontario and arrived in time to spend some time with him. He was strong. At times they thought he was gone, then he would rally again.

On Sunday morning, June 16, at 4:50 a.m., the last line of the last page, of the last chapter, of the book of the life of Jacob Johann Friesen was written, and with his last sigh, its covers quietly closed. His pilgrimage was ended.

Since it was Sunday, those family members present could only notify the relatives at a distance and prepare to entertain them when they arrived.

They would have to wait for the bank to open on Monday to access the funeral plans that were in safekeeping there, the plans prepared by Justina eighteen years earlier. All were notified, except Carl and Vera Hansen and family, who were somewhere on their way from California, where they had finished ten months of studies at Fuller Theological Seminary. They were expected to arrive in a few days' time. But that evening they arrived ahead of schedule. Others continued to arrive from Ontario, Pennsylvania, and Saskatchewan.

The funeral was held on Thursday, June 20, 1985, in the Duchess Mennonite Church. The funeral plans were followed, except that Charles Ramer preached the sermon since C.J. Ramer was no longer able. Many people filled the church, and over 200 stayed for lunch afterwards. There was a downpour of rain as he was being interred in the Duchess Cemetery, just next to his faithful companion of forty-eight years. At the lunch following interment, the German speakers present sang the song, "Take Thou My Hand Oh Father!", the song that was sung at their farewell when they left their home in Russia sixty-one years earlier.

> *All these people were still living by faith when they died. They did not receive the things promised; they only saw them and welcomed them from a distance. And they admitted that they were aliens and strangers on earth. People who say such things show that they are looking for a country of their own. If they had been thinking of the country they had left, they would have had opportunity to return. Instead, they were longing for a better country—a heavenly one. Therefore, God is not ashamed to be called their God, for he has prepared a city for them!* – Hebrews 11:13-16 NIV
>
> *I saw the Holy City, the new Jerusalem, coming down out of heaven from God, prepared as a bride beautifully dressed for her husband. And I heard a loud voice from the throne saying, "Now the dwelling of God is with men, and he will live with them. They will be his people, and God himself will be with them and be their God. He will wipe every tear from their eyes. There will be no more death or mourning or crying or pain, for the old order of things has passed away ... To him who is thirsty*

I will give to drink without cost from the spring of the water of life. He who overcomes will inherit all this, and I will be his God and he will be my child." – Revelation 21:2-4, 6-7 NIV

Duchess Cemetery with Warkentin, Friesen, & Hansen Grave Markers

Appendix

The Diaspora of the Tribe of Jacob and Justina

"The Friesen Fourteen," "The Tribe of Jacob and Justina" at a Family Reunion in 1978, l. to r. from oldest to youngest: Elizabeth Hansen, Jacob Friesen, Neta Broadfoot, Hedy Friesen, Tena Friesen, Helen Biehn, Melita Grove, Anita Dyck, Annie Roth, Susan Friesen, Edward Friesen, Martha Derbecker, Esther Visser, and David Friesen.

In the years following the completion of Justina's pilgrimage, during the prolonged hospitalization and ultimate passing of Jacob, and the subsequent years, what happened in the lives of their offspring, the "*Friesen Fourteen,*" sometimes referred to as the "*Tribe of Jacob*"? Every human being is worthy and has a story that has potential for being the subject of a good book. The life stories of each of these fourteen is no exception. However, such a task would be too complicated for this author.

Let me give a summary of the lives of each of them, my much-loved and revered aunts and uncles, my fellow pilgrims. As of this writing, in 2022, for all except two, Martha and David, their milliseconds on this earth have expired, their personal pilgrimages completed. They have entered their rest.

In the fall of 1969 Jens and Elizabeth Hansen sold their farm machinery to their youngest son, Charles, and retired from farming. Jens found a job at a school in Brooks as grounds man in the spring of 1970. He worked there for the next five years full time, then for two more summers until he retired completely in the fall of 1977 at seventy-three years of age.

They bought a lot in Duchess and constructed a basement upon which a new modular home was installed. This made a very comfortable retirement home into which they moved on New Year's Day, 1974. Charles and Freda continued to live with them, until they both married two and three years later.

Gradually, creeping age stole Jens's health and his powers to help himself. He developed diabetes, his hearing went almost completely, his eyes degenerated, and by November 1984, he, being no longer able to walk, was admitted to the Brooks Auxiliary Hospital, a nursing home, where he remained under nursing care, for seven years and three months, until he passed away on February 6th, 1992, just eleven days before his eighty-eighth birthday.

Completing fifty-three years of marriage, Elizabeth now continued to live alone in their home in Duchess enjoying a comfortable retirement, tending her garden, entertaining her grandchildren, and hosting "Coffee Bible studies" with friends. In the fall of 2004, at age eighty-four, she moved into the Newbrook Lodge in Brooks. After a few years under nursing care at Sunrise Gardens, she passed away in her sleep on February 22, 2019.

At the time of her passing at ninety-eight and one-half years of age, she had been predeceased by her parents, her husband, Jens, one granddaughter, Kathy, and eleven siblings. She was survived by one brother, David, and one sister, Martha. Together, Jens and Elizabeth raised seven children who all survive: Peter/Margret Hansen, Carl/Vera Hansen, Paul/Irene Hansen, George/Marilyn Hansen, Charles/Wynona Hansen, Linda Hansen, and Freda/Tom King. Also surviving were twenty-five grandchildren, fifty-two great grandchildren and fourteen great great grandchildren.

Jake and Wilma raised eight children: Ronald, Marilyn, Lily, Richard, Judy, Darrell, Patricia, and Steven. In September 1973, Jake and Wilma moved from Duchess with their younger children to Emo in northwest Ontario, where they bought a dairy farm. There the remaining children grew up and went on their own.

They sold their farm in September 1987, and again moved, this time to Hague, Saskatchewan. There they bought a dryland farm and farmed for two more years. Riding the tractor was getting too difficult for Jake, so they moved back to Duchess, in 1991, where they bought George Hansen's farm and lived there for some years. Their son Richard did the farming.

In their later years, Jake and Wilma moved into an apartment built onto their daughter and son-in-law, Judy, and Frank Bear's house. There, Jake took care of Wilma as she battled the effects of Alzheimer's disease until she passed away on November 30, 2005. Jake passed away on September 21, 2007, aged eighty-five.

Jake had served as a deacon and on financial committees. He also taught Christian business ethics and dealt with problems in their church. Jake and Wilma had thirty-eight grandchildren and numerous great grandchildren at the time of their passing.

Neta and Jack Broadfoot moved a better house onto their farm near Watrous, Saskatchewan and retired there. Their eldest son, David, passed away in 2013. The rest of their six sons, Andrew, Roderick, Donavan, Kenneth, and Laurence, have married and there are seven grandchildren. Jack passed away on November 24, 2008, aged eighty-six years of age. Neta died on December 24, 2013, being aged eighty-nine years.

Hedy retired in 1991. She lived in one of the senior citizen's apartments in Duchess. She spent her time writing letters, drinking coffee with her friends, running around in her little white Dodge, and entertaining grand nieces and nephews. She took upon herself the task of being the family's record keeper, producing a periodic update of the growing family tree.

In late 1994, she became very ill with cancer, but with treatment, made a remarkable recovery. In 1997, the cancer returned, and on Wednesday,

January 28, 1998, Hedy passed away in the Brooks Hospital, aged seventy-two years. Her funeral was held in the Duchess Mennonite Church and her mortal remains were interred in the Duchess Cemetery.

Tena passed away on October 1, 1991, in her apartment in Ottawa after a lengthy battle with cancer. At sixty-four years of age, she was the first of the Friesen Fourteen to pass on. At her request, she was cremated, and her ashes were interred in the Duchess cemetery. A memorial service was conducted for her in the Duchess Mennonite Church.

In 1993, Helen and Mervin retired into a new house they built for themselves on their farm near Moorefield, Ontario. Their son, Edwin, took over the farming operation. They lived there for four years. They were getting involved in a ministry to the Old Colony Mennonites that were migrating back to Canada from Mexico. Many of them were settling around the Moorefield area. These immigrants were very needy materially as well as spiritually. Since Helen was able to communicate with them in the Plattdeutsch language, she could be a great help to them.

On December 12, 1995, Mervin and Helen had just made a call on a young couple in Rothsay. As they were driving onto the main road, their car was struck by a large truck. Helen was killed instantly. She was almost sixty-seven years of age. Mervin was hospitalized but recuperated. In his later years, he moved in with his daughter, Bernice, and her husband, Clayton Gingerich, as he suffered the debilitating effects of Parkinson's disease. He passed on February 16, 2007, in Palmerston, Ontario.

They were married for forty-seven years and raised five sons and one daughter, Roy, Bernice, Edwin, Vernon, Myron, and Laverne. They had twenty-one grandchildren. Roy and his wife Miriam spent several years as missionary volunteers in Guatemala. Edwin was ordained to the Christian ministry on December 2, 1990, for service in the Woodlawn Mennonite Church.

Even though they officially retired to their home in Duchess, John and Melita Grove were active doing volunteer work wherever they were needed. They worked in such diverse places as doing hospital maintenance for a mission in Haiti, directing a Mennonite Disaster Service unit in cleaning up after a flood in Colorado, building church buildings, organizing, and preparing for Mennonite Relief Sales, helping their children, Steve, and Debra Lantz, building homes for the poor with Habitat for Humanity in

Texas, plus innumerable little errands of mercy for family members and neighbors.

A lasting monument to John's memory was the construction of several church buildings, including ones at Duchess, Vauxhall, and Tofield.

A son, Joe Grove was killed in a head on collision, when the car he was driving met another speeding car on the brow of a hill on a narrow gravel country road at 2:00 a.m. in 1973. At age seventeen, he was the first of the Friesen clan to meet an untimely death since the family's arrival in Canada in 1924.

Their daughter, Debra Lantz, died of cancer on January 29, 2001. The remaining sons, Gordon, Albert, and Tom raised their families in the Brooks/Duchess community. John and Melita had eleven grandchildren.

Melita suffered for several years with the lung condition, pulmonary fibrosis, which eventually took her life on January 1, 2012, in Medicine Hat, Alberta. She was eighty-two. Her husband, John Grove spent his last years in Sunrise Gardens where he passed away, aged ninety-three, during the COVID-19 epidemic in 2020.

Anita and Jake Dyck lived in Brooks. After a busy career of construction work, Jake retired. Both suffered different health issues. Jake passed away on July 16, 2010, aged eighty-two. Anita died on October 14, 2013, aged eighty-one. They raised two adopted children, Connie, and Glen, and had three grandchildren.

In 1973, Lyle and Annie Roth purchased the Roth home farm near Kingman, Alberta, after his folks passed away. There they took up dairy farming and finished raising their family of four sons, Arthur, Curtis, Victor, and Robin, and one daughter, Verlene. In 1990, they sold the farm to son Victor and his wife, Charlene, who built a new house on it. Lyle worked for a machine dealer in Camrose for some years.

He had quadruple bypass surgery done in July 1997. He recuperated well. In their advanced years, both were admitted to nursing homes in Camrose. Annie suffered from Parkinson's disease and died on November 19, 2012, aged eighty. Lyle suffered from dementia and passed away a few years later. They had twelve grandchildren.

Susan lived her adult life alone in Kitchener, Ontario. Upon reaching her retirement age, her health was not good. Her interests include family history. Afflicted with cancer, she passed away on December 6, 2009, aged seventy-four years.

In 1974, Edward took a new job with Redline Implements of Fairview to work as a supervisor in the Ford department. He found the job to be quite stressful and decided to make a change accepting a position with the Fairview College in 1980 as a college fleet mechanic. His wife, Faye, took a job at the E.E. Oliver School in Fairview as a teacher's aide. She worked there for seventeen years. They were active members of the Bluesky Mennonite Church.

Ed was compelled to take an early retirement, in 1984, due to the debilitating effects of Parkinson's disease. In May 1991 he and Faye sold their home in Fairview and moved to Edmonton to be nearer to family and medical expertise. They bought a condominium in a retirement village in Mill Woods, half a block away from his sister and brother-in-law, Esther and John Visser who had also bought into that village. On April 29, 1999, Ed passed away. He was sixty-three years old. Faye is still living in Edmonton. Their three children, Patricia, Sherilyn, and Kenton, all got university degrees and have scattered to successful careers. They had five grandchildren.

Martha was remarried to Earl Derbecker in 1989. They managed a thrift shop in the Hanover-Walkerton, Ontario, area. Earl died on August 9, 1998. Martha since moved to Kitchener, Ontario, and still lives there alone. Her daughter, Marianne, lives with her husband, David Timbury and three adult children in Elmira, Ontario. Her other daughter, Valerie, lives in Newport News, Virginia, with her husband, David Schaefer and two adult children.

Esther and John also have passed on. In 1997, John had a hip replacement which enforced his retired status. He also had kidney problems and high blood pressure. He died on January 4, 2009, aged eighty years. Esther suffered for years with recurrent cancer and died a year and a half later, September 13, 2010, aged sixty-nine. They had two grandchildren.

Following their two-year sojourn in Illinois, David and Esther returned to Pennsylvania where he resumed pursuing his accounting career. He worked full time, while studying on the side, and raising a family, and being active in church and community. Some fifteen years later, he graduated with a degree in his chosen field while working as chief accountant for Ralph's Supermarket. He then worked as the financial head for the Clemens chain of some twelve supermarkets.

Their children, Brian, and Gayle, both graduated from college, married well, and are gainfully employed. Their five grandchildren, Emily, Joanna, Josiah, Brianna, and Sonya are now adults and doing well.

On one of their many trips back to Alberta to visit David's roots, they stopped to visit the Russian Mennonite Museum in Steinbach, Manitoba. This inspired David to re-connect with his Russian Mennonite roots in a fresh way. They celebrated their 25th wedding anniversary by traveling to the Netherlands and Germany where they met some of David's cousins who had migrated from Ischalka, Samara, Russia.

In March 1993, David and his wife, Esther, joined nine other members of Mennonite Economic Development Associates (MEDA) on a trip to Moscow where they presented a seminar on retailing in America to about sixty owners and managers of newly privatized retail stores in that city.

In a sense, though Jacob and Justina's farewell to Russia and family there was final, in David's contacts, the circle was at least symbolically restored. Since that time, other family members have also made that trip to Germany to renew family ties with their many Russian-born cousins.

As of July 1, 2017, the Jacob and Justina Friesen family tree included 497 persons. Of this total, 378 were direct descendants including a few adoptions. The remainder were spouses. Of the total, 472 were living and twenty-five had passed on.

Printed in the United States
by Baker & Taylor Publisher Services